30p

REMEMBERI

CW01619504

As a close frienc r
Sellers for many ye e
unique position to write the real story of the man as well as the actor.

From the public house in London where the Goon Shows were born, the golden days of radio and variety, to his involvements with some of the world's most glamorous women, this intimate memoir is packed with anecdotes which reveal the many and often surprising sides of the chameleon Sellers—a man whose own character was as complex and diverse as the legendary screen characters he created.

REMEMBERING PETER SELLERS

Graham Stark

Lansdown
CHIVERS·PRESS·BATH

First published in Great Britain 1990
by
Robson Books Ltd
This Large Print edition published by
Chivers Press
by arrangement with
Robson Books Ltd
1992

ISBN 0 7451 5551 0

British Library Cataloguing in Publication Data available

Photoset, printed and bound in Great Britain by
REDWOOD PRESS LIMITED, Melksham, Wiltshire

To Audrey

LOUISE, the coloured housekeeper, looks at CHANCE, the gardener.

LOUISE:

You're always going to be a little boy, ain't you?

She kisses him on the cheek.

Goodbye, Chance.

LOUISE exits.

(*Dialogue excerpt from the film* Being There, *starring Peter Sellers.*)

CONTENTS

FOREWORD

In the years since Peter Seller's death in 1980 interest in him has never waned. If anything, it has strengthened. My friendship with him was fairly public knowledge, and to this day reporters still ask about past incidents, film buffs pursue with enquiries, and a few months ago a playwright sent an exhaustive list of questions as he was writing about an incident in Peter's life. As he was recommended by Alan Ayckbourn I agreed to help but, generally speaking, I have become wary. Several years ago I did agree to talk at some length about Peter, then found the anecdotes were used in a book which seemed to me, sadly, so biased that I regretted my collaboration.

Ten years is the first anniversary with the zero on the end and perhaps is as good a time as any to recount the mostly delightful, sometimes hysterical, occasionally sad, experiences that Peter and I had together. On a shelf in my study is a row of diaries dating from 1951 up to the present day. They cover the entire time I spent working with Peter and have proved to be a wonderfully accurate means of recalling the extraordinary times we spent together. I owe this book to those diaries.

It is not a biography. It is a recounting of

incidents I shared with someone who is still remembered with affection throughout the world. Three years ago I was flown to Malaysia to give some lectures on photography. The first was in Singapore, the audience consisting entirely of Chinese photographers. The ice was broken, and all fears I had about communicating with them removed, as one of the Chinese gentlemen in the front row stood up, pointed a finger at me and exclaimed, 'Ah. Prink Pranther!' At least that's what it sounded like!

The fascination with Peter is world-wide, but it's local too as I still meet smiling faces at the newsagent's, who give me a nudge and say, 'Saw you on the box in that *Panther* last night. Cor, that Peter Sellers must have been a bit of a one. I could see you was 'avin a good time.'

Well, he was a bit of a one, and we did have a good time. These are my memories of that good time.

CHAPTER ONE

WE RODE THROUGH THE WAR ON A CREST OF A WAVE

Early on the morning of 24 July 1980, Peter Sellers died. The evening before, I'd sat amongst an invited audience at the Empire Cinema, Leicester Square, watching the London première of Alan Parker's film *Fame*.

The location of the movie was the streets of New York where, years ago, Peter and I had walked, gazing up open-mouthed at those huge skyscrapers that, up to then, we'd only seen in the movies. Like two schoolboys we'd larked about at the top of the Empire State Building, two idiotic actors pretending to be King Kong, snarling realistically at imaginary fighter planes. Jokingly we'd done a bit of a soft shoe on Park Avenue along with Jules Munshin, who was the third sailor in that classic film musical *On The Town*, Pete and I deputizing for Gene Kelly and Frank Sinatra. We even took the tourist trip round the Statue of Liberty.

The papers had made light of the fact Pete had gone to hospital, except one brief mention, in an evening paper, that rumoured a life-support machine was being used.

I looked at those New York scenes and got a

nasty feeling in my stomach. To a roar of applause the screening ended. The picture was a smash hit. I'd been sitting next to Ernie Wise, and as we started to leave the circle he asked me if I was going on to the disco première party at Victoria. I've never believed in extra-sensory perception, but some hunch or other just told me this wasn't the night to go dancing so off home I went.

At four o'clock in the morning the bedside phone woke me. It was Peter's son, Michael Sellers. Considering what he was saying, his voice was really quite steady. 'Hello, Graham. I thought you ought to be one of the first to know ... I'm afraid the old man didn't make it ... I didn't want you to find out any other way.' I thanked him for his thoughtfulness, mumbled the cliché consolations, got out of bed, made a cup of tea, and gave a silent toast to the memory of Leading Aircraftman P. Sellers, late of His Majesty's Royal Air Force and my best friend for most of the thirty-five years I'd known him.

Toasting Peter in a cup of tea seemed rather apt as he wallowed in the memories of those early Air Force days and loved to talk of the times when those two brave boys in blue, LAC Sellers and Sergeant Stark, hair slicked down with Brylcreem, buttons shining like cats' eyes, and with creases in their uniform trousers you could sharpen a pencil with, made nightly sorties on the famous service club, the Nuffield

Centre off Piccadilly. Sorties that would have done credit to Air Marshall 'Bomber' Harris. The war had just ended, we were waiting to be demobbed, and we both felt it was about time we got rid of all those pimples that the terrible Service food had given us.

From the balcony overlooking the dance floor, we scrutinized every WAAF, WREN and ATS girl in sight, our own personal radar rejecting all the non-starters, the highly improbables, and anything with a higher rank than sergeant. After all, it's one thing saying, 'What about it, darling?' It's quite another saying, 'What about it, Sir?' We simply concentrated on what we, in our inexperience, hoped might be what was known in the services as dead certs.

I must admit neither of us could have been described as matineé idols. In fact, in those days, Peter was inclined to be rather plump, a bit moonfaced, and his short-sightedness made him screw up his eyes. As for me, well I could be best described as a skinny Mr Punch, with just a touch of Stan Laurel; nevertheless, we did all right. We vaguely hinted at past secret missions successfully accomplished, and the fact that we'd both been in the famous RAF Gang Show didn't do any harm. We managed to get our fair share of pretty girls back to Peter's flat and, after conveniently getting rid of his dear mother Peg, the lights would be lowered and on went the music.

Even in those days gadgets held sway over Peter and he was the first person I knew who actually owned an automatic record player. You loaded eight heavy 78 r.p.m. records onto this monster machine and switched on. The first record slid down the centre pillar, hit the turntable with a horrendous clonk, an enormous needle arm swung over and after a bit of a scratchy start you were off for half an hour of uninterrupted, boyish, bobbysox idol Frank Sinatra. After lots of experiments with mood music like Axel Stordahl and his strings and Glenn Miller (only playing the slow numbers), we found Frankie seemed to be the key to success. However, we were realists. If surrender hadn't come by record five we gave up. Mind you, Peter didn't only depend on what the music might do. Fantasy always played a big part with him and he assured all the ladies he was a direct descendant of Lord Nelson. He half convinced me, although I could never understand how a link with one arm and a lost eye could possibly help your sex life.

Pete and I had met, quite by chance, at the headquarters of the RAF Gang Show, which was stationed in a building in Houghton Street, just off Aldwych, now occupied by the London School of Economics. Taken over by the RAF for the duration of the war, it had a marvellous little theatre which made it a natural for the units which Ralph Reader, the pre-war brain behind the famous Scout Gang Shows, had mustered for the Air Force. He was made a squadron leader, and organised thirteen all-male shows and two all-WAAF (Women's Auxiliary Air Force) shows. The sexual segregation may have been unjust but if you're sending shows into the front line I suppose it was a wise decision. Anyway, like the rest of the service, we manfully accepted the bromide in the tea, ran around the camp perimeter a lot, and made sure we didn't talk about sex too much in the barrack room at night. Gloomy lectures by the Medical Officers about venereal disease didn't have too much effect but, sensibly, they also showed full-colour medical pictures of unfortunate sufferers of said diseases, which did.

* * *

All the shows had long service abroad. Peter, in no. 10 unit, did his share in the Far East, but was mainly in European theatres of war. My unit, no. 4, went to Algiers, Italy, the Middle East. We then played to almost every single RAF Station in India, finishing up by being flown into the famous siege of Imphal, in Burma, while it was still surrounded by the Japanese. Typical of the services, the nearer the front line, the better the audience. Like most of the service shows, there being no females in the cast, we spent quite a few scenes dressed to the nines as ladies.

In May 1945, VE day had come and gone and the gangsters had either killed themselves or been rounded up to await their fate in Nuremberg. We were still rather aptly singing 'We're Riding Along On The Crest Of A Wave' (the theme song of the Gang Show) while being drowned in monsoons in Burma. Finally, our tour of duty was over and the troop ship took us back to Europe just in time to cross the Rhine to see for ourselves the devastation that had been wreaked on Germany. Maybe I felt a touch of sympathy until Celle, North Germany.

During an afternoon show, in a huge circus tent, we were forced to open the rear flaps of the tent in the dressing room area as the sun was high and it was baking hot. Rushing through a quick change, I was busy putting on a comedy make-up when I suddenly became aware of two little girls, hand in hand, gazing at me with their large, dark eyes wide open. They stood just outside the tent, angelic, hardly believing what they were looking at. The strange man in the funny suit, plastering his face with white make-up. They couldn't have been more than four or five and were identically dressed in the clothes that the occupying authorities were giving to the thousands of displaced persons they found wandering the countryside. Their little dresses were gingham, with pretty little puffed sleeves swelling out at the top of their bare arms, and on the inside of each of their left bare arms was tattooed a long number. I never knew whether they were Jewish or gypsy. I only know that the image of those two little innocent children, marked for life, has never left my memory.

Then all our lives changed. On 6 August 1945 the 'Enola Gay' climbed into the sky, in its bomb bay the nine-foot cylinder called 'Little Boy', heading for Hiroshima. Within a few days it was all over. In Piccadilly we danced, sang, made idiots of ourselves, realizing that at last we'd actually won. The cowboys in the white hats had come charging over the hill and had defeated the baddies.

In the Gang Shows I'd played alongside many fellow airmen like Tony Hancock, and Dick Emery, who later became big successes in show business, but I did not actually meet Peter until the last few weeks of my time in the RAF. He was doing his fair share of shows abroad alongside someone in his unit who became a lifelong friend to both of us, and a fellow actor in movies, David Lodge. While I was in Germany, Peter was living up to the title I gave him very early on in our friendship, namely Golden Bollocks, by getting on an incredible posting, for a time, in the South of France. To say nature looked on him kindly was an understatement. Time and again he defied fate by always falling on his feet and, if I was around to observe this phenomenon, I would give an unbelieving shake of the head and, to Pete's great delight, mouth carefully those two words.

At last, like the rest of the units, I was in London, filling in time waiting for my demobilization. Hanging round headquarters for, and yet strangely dreading, the return to civvy street. The comforting umbrella of the service, which controlled every move you made, would soon be furled and stuck away just in your memory. A living, in a strange new world, would have to be made.

Many of the older men, especially those who were married, were demobbed as soon as possible. This meant I'd been made a sergeant for no better reason than, as most of my unit had gone back to civilian life, someone had to be promoted. Establishment was the name of the Air Force game and if there wasn't a sergeant to be found a sergeant would have to be created. I rather fancied the three stripes on my arm, if for nothing else than to be called 'Sarge' instead of 'Oi yew!'

The small turning where our headquarters were, Houghton Street, was invariably deserted as petrol rationing was still in force, and what few cars there were had all the empty main roads of London to park in. One warm, sunny afternoon I walked down the steps of the building to see a car parked by the kerb. This event was noticeable for several reasons. Firstly, it was the only car I'd ever seen parked in that street; secondly, the car was very large, black, and American; and thirdly, it was being polished by a young, somewhat diffident leading aircraftman.

The whole thing had an air of a sequence from a Hitchcock movie. The empty street, the incongruous car, the lone airman silently polishing. Round eyes behind horn-rimmed glasses seriously studied the chrome emblem on the bonnet. He breathed hard on it, giving it a loving polish with a yellow cloth. Then he saw me and gave a nod and a grin. 'Only does fourteen to the gallon but you've got to admit it's a right beauty'. No concern with petrol rationing, no concern that I was a sergeant. He just wasn't impressed. In future times one of the great delights I found in Peter was his absolute disregard for whatever august position people might occupy. Princes, presidents, or producers were all the same to Peter. Either he liked them or he didn't. A simple behaviour pattern which was extremely endearing in a profession which has its fair share of sycophants.

No one's ever been able to explain why, out of the thousands of people you meet, you become friends with one particular person. I only know that from the moment we met, Pete and I were friends. Maybe we saw in each other someone we could confide in, maybe it was because we laughed at the same things, or maybe it was because it was so obvious he didn't give a sod whether I was a sergeant or not.

Fortunately for us English airmen, nearby was one of those small tea shops, beloved of the British. The large steaming dispenser of boiling water greeted you as soon as you entered. The café owner expertly pulled the control lever towards him, clouds of hissing steam briefly blotted him from view, then thick, white, porcelain cups, always brimming over with tea, were slid across the tiled top of the counter. All for the price of a penny a cup. As the going rate from His Majesty the King for an airman was four shillings and sixpence a day you had to think about things like that. Mind you, my sergeant's stripes had given me a bit of a rise so the tea, that day, was down to me.

Yes, Pete and I had decided that a tea break was essential so that we could sit and go through the necessary preliminary skirmishing of a budding friendship. From the word go we hit it off, and across the table we swapped stories of the extraordinary exploits we'd both got up to in the Gang Shows. I got in the one about trying to give a show in Naples while Vesuvius was in full eruption. Pete topped that with his account of how Dave Lodge and he had managed to get petrol for their truck by smuggling jerry cans of petrol under their greatcoats, staggering through the streets at night like two gross Billy Bunters with every chance of being on sick parade in the morning with severe hernias.

Potted histories came next, and I heard about Peter and his parents and their dalliance with the fringes of show business. Then, to round off our first meeting I got a taste of Peter's sudden, impulsive generosity. Having learnt that my mother had died early in the war, my two brothers were still abroad with the army, and my father was wallowing about on the Atlantic Ocean as an officer in the Merchant Navy, Pete's eyes narrowed and he peered a bit closer. 'Where do you sleep then?'

With a mixture of off-handedness and embarrassment I explained that my present abode was Rowton House, the famous lodging house opposite Waterloo Station, home to many of the sad tramps who otherwise would have wandered the streets of London. One shilling a night is what it cost to doss down in their dormitory, and all was well providing you took the precaution of lifting the end of your metal bed then put the legs back down again, this time inside your empty shoes. This guarded against the nasty habit of some of the inmates of stealing your service shoes. A fair price could be obtained for them on the black market. To prevent your uniform disappearing during the night was equally simple. You merely folded it and put it under your mattress. The trousers creases were fine but it didn't do a lot for your battledress top. Shirts, underpants and socks were slept in. It was a bit rough but I didn't have much option.

'Gawd Almighty,' was the expression Pete used when I told him and at once he was calling his home. Before I knew what was happening I got a ride in the American car up to East Finchley, where I met his parents, Peg and Bill, for the first time. I was taken to the flat directly beneath them (they lived on the top floor), where I was faced by a plump, motherly matron who was obviously a close friend of the Sellerses. Peter gave a performance which was deserving of some sort of award.

Here was an airman, he dramatically told the lady, bereft of motherly love, lately returned from facing the foe in the jungles of Burma, yet forced to sleep in nightly squalor, and what about that spare room you've got as I'm sure you could do with the rent he will be only too glad to pay! Bravura was not the word. Ever so slightly moist eyes blinked as the lady told me to collect what luggage I had and return immediately. So there it was. No more fastening down the shoes, no more crumpled uniform, and I wallowed in the luxury of a hot bath into which, sentiment or not, my new landlady had discreetly poured a large measure of disinfectant.

CHAPTER TWO

PEG OF MY HEART

To write about Peter and not to write of his mother, Peg, would be like writing about Laurel without Hardy, except that it wasn't that comical. Tiny, bird-like, with darting looks from her big dark eyes, she seemed to be constantly scanning the immediate area that surrounded her son as if expecting something to harm him. She attempted to weave a protective screen around him. Any male friend of Peter's was fine (she seemed to like me a lot) but she had a blind spot about any woman that came within ten feet of her boy. And boy was the operative word. Peg wouldn't, and couldn't, permit Peter to grow old in her eyes. He was her whole being, her whole life, and when they were together she never took her eyes off him. She followed every movement. Peg wasn't really interested in Peter's success; in a way she didn't like it as it took him away from her. There was no hint of theatrical mum, and isn't my boy the best. From the first time I met her with Peter, I realized this was a relationship that would have made Dr Freud rub his hands with glee. I don't think Krafft-Ebing would have been uninterested either.

Peter's father, Bill, I never got to know. Bland and faceless, he merged into the background, giving total centre stage to Peg. He nodded agreement with every remark made and, apparently, was obsessed with not making waves. That is, if anyone quite so nebulous could be obsessed. Even now it's difficult to conjure up a mental picture of him. He seemed to exist in a private world of peace at any price, particularly where Peg was concerned, and it's some indication of their relationship that you never thought of them as husband and wife, only as Bill and Peg.

Peg was the one who supplied the car Peter first drove me in, and the petrol to run it. God knows what strings she must have pulled to get it, especially in those days, but her Peter was going to have it. Many years later, after both she and Peter had died, I had a nostalgic meeting with the administrative squadron leader who ran the Gang Show office in London, Jack Cracknell. In an unguarded moment, he told me how Peg had haunted him, offering any inducement to stop Peter getting an overseas posting. I'm sure if Peter had known he would have been furious. He'd have missed all that fun in Paris and the South of France. Peter was often embarrassed by Peg but he knew how desperately she loved him, knew how many sacrifices she'd made for him in the early days, and tried his best to keep her happy by humouring her.

After a few weeks of Finchley and the disinfectant baths I altered the direction Horace Greeley gave and headed north, getting my first post-war job, as an actor in a repertory company based in Coventry. Well, Peter's help could only go so far. I had to earn a living and I had the chance of being in a Christmas production of *Alice in Wonderland*. I told Pete I'd see him soon, thanked him kindly, and off I went to get dressed up in an animal skin to play the Gryphon. I only went for one production but they seemed to be very impressed with the comic business I invented with my tail, and asked me to stay on. Four years later I left the company and returned to London, a lot more experienced as an actor but not a lot richer.

The strange force known as coincidence then took a hand as Tony Hancock, with whom I'd worked in the Gang Show, lurched back into my life. Sadly, lurched is the operative word, as Tony was always rather partial to the bottle. Nevertheless he was the funniest comedian I ever saw or worked with. Finding that I was living in a damp Dickensian basement room in Holland Park, he felt, as Peter had done just after the war, that Graham needed help. In passing, grubby journalists and seedy pundits often have a field day mocking actors for their vanity, their jealousies, their hysterics, but nobody ever seems to talk about their generosity. Mention a charity and they'll give up their Sundays, have a worthy social cause and they'll carry a banner all day, and, to my own knowledge, they will never see a fellow actor starve. Their generosity of behaviour should be an example to all those people who mock them, but I don't suppose for a moment it ever will be. Hancock's reaction to the basement room was just the same as Peter's to Rowton House. The only difference was that times had progressed and instead of saying 'Gawd Almighty!', Tony said 'Christ Almighty!'

Anyway, just like Peter, Tony did the decent thing, and helped by fixing for me to meet a BBC radio producer, convincing him I was the right person to join Hancock in a new radio show he was doing. Peter Butterworth, Bill Kerr and I joined the lad himself in a four-handed Scout sketch in a show headed by Derek Roy. The show was so-so, but the BBC realized it had a future star in Hancock and moved him, along with myself, into a new series. It was an instant hit and I was launched on a career in radio. The Gang Show brotherhood, forged on several hundred rickety stages, continued to look after its own.

All the time I was away in repertory Peter was going through the hell of the struggling performer. A stint as a fairground barker, working in a holiday camp, even being booked in second-rate music halls as a star drummer. He tried it all. In later years, when the mood took me, I would make him tell me about his début as 'Britain's answer to Gene Krupa' at the Aldershot Hippodrome. As a story of total and absolute disaster it unfailingly reduced me to tears of laughter. Peter's idea was that he would sit behind his drums, high on a rostrum, in total darkness, while the pit orchestra began the music. Dramatically a single spot would be focused just on Peter's hands, gradually widening while he drove the audience to a frenzy of delight with his drum virtuosity. Well, that was the idea anyway. In practice things were a bit different. They didn't have rostrums so he had to make do with shaky tea chests, the electrician was drunk so the spot shone straight into the audience's eyes, blinding them, and the full orchestra (three players only) were four bars behind after the first thirty seconds.

But Peter persevered and even came out relatively unscathed from a stint at the legendary Windmill Theatre ('we never clothed') doing six shows a day. The horror of appearing on that tiny stage, purely filling in while the girls unclothed themselves for yet another tableau, scarred many a hardened comic, but Peter managed to survive, and if you could survive that you could survive anything.

In 1951, a few weeks before I got back to

London, he met, and married, Anne Hayes. She was a very young and beautiful actress and was the love of his life. By then he'd started to make his mark in radio and was currently appearing in *Ray's a laugh*, starring Ted Ray, one of the most successful BBC half-hour shows. The day after I'd started working with Hancock the phone went. 'Gra, it's Pete. Any chance of you coming over and meeting Anne?' In their flat overlooking the Hyde Park I met Anne for the first time, highly approved of her (I think it was mutual) and then found out what the real reason for the phone call was. Peter's enthusiasm for his fellow actors never died. Time and time again he would see a performance, like it, and then devote a lot of energy to seeing that performance was noted by every producer and director he knew. At the height of his fame he was in the audience one night watching the four young, unknown performers in *Beyond the Fringe*, Peter Cook, Dudley Moore, Alan Bennett and Jonathan Miller. He launched a publicity campaign on their behalf which had to be seen to be believed.

I sat in the flat that night and Peter looked at me. 'Heard you with Hancock last night. You're a bleeding natural, you are. Must make a phone call.' There and then, without any preamble, he called the private number of George Inns, producer of *Ray's A Laugh*. 'George,' he said. 'I know we need a replacement in the show, and I've got just the boy.' So, on 1 January 1952, I sat in an office at the BBC, palms wet with nerves, having to read an audition script in front of one of the greatest performers in radio, Ted Ray. Luckily he liked me and two days later, I performed in my first *Ray's A Laugh* and worked alongside Peter professionally for the first time.

To be a 'character man' in radio in those days meant that if you were lucky enough to sight-read well, and had the facility to conjure up dozens of 'character voices', you could join the circle of performers who formed the backbone of all the famous light entertainment shows that were so popular. Among them were Kenneth Connor, Kenneth Williams, Jon Pertwee, but leading the field was Peter. Every other 'voice man', as we were also called, acknowledged that he was in a class of his own. Maybe there were characters more popular than the ones he invented but nobody had his particular vocal facility. However talented, you somehow could never quite disguise your own basic voice—but Peter, through some freak of nature, could. If he wanted, he could talk to you, his closest friend, on the telephone, and you would never know it was him.

In the early 1960s, during the satire boom, using film clips of famous figures was all the rage. Peter was booked by a major advertising company to put voices on such clips of Nikita

Kruschev, President Kennedy and Prime Minister Macmillan. Their voices were already on the film excerpts but the sense could be slightly changed, and this was to be the basis for a comedy compilation. Young director Bernie Stringle, already famous for the legendary PG Tips chimp commercials, which Peter and I both put voices to, was in charge of the recording. Peter duly arrived and, in the space of half an hour, gave perfect impressions of Kruschev, Kennedy and Macmillan. The next day the tapes were played back for editing purposes and it was found that they'd been mixed up. Peter's voice match was so perfect on all three men that, until the tapes were fully replayed, and the change of dialogue discovered, they could not ascertain which was real, and which was Peter's impression.

Ray's A Laugh was great fun mainly because of Ted. To see him perform a script at the microphone was to watch a maestro at work. He had the justified reputation of having the quickest wit in show business. He was honoured one year by being elected by his fellow Water Rats (the all-comedian charity) as King Rat, thereby sitting at the head of the table at their annual dinner. The red-coated Toast Master (like so many of them, an ex-regimental sergeant-major) roared at the assembled company that now Mr Ted Ray would say grace. Shuffling to their feet, almost every famous comedian in the country stood, head bowed, while Ted muttered the 'for what we are about to receive' formula. At once the Toast Master roared again. 'Speak up, Mr Ray, can't hear you!' Without a pause Ted looked at him and said, 'I wasn't talking to you.' No wonder Peter and I adored him.

But one night I think we both went a bit too far. During rehearsals Ted was telling us about his amorous exploits with some barmaid in the north of England. He was a great story teller and we were almost crying with laughter as he took out his pocket handkerchief and tucked it under his chin, likc a scrviette, to illustrate some quite appalling sexual antic he and the barmaid had got up to. *Ray's A Laugh* was a 'live' radio show and that night, while Ted was at the microphone, Pete and I moved either side of him, ready for a short scene, both of us with our handkerchiefs tucked under our chins. The producer was baffled, the stuio audience was baffled, and the twenty-three million listeners were even more baffled as Ted took one look at us and became hysterical with laughter. He really couldn't stop. That story was to have a finale that neither Ted, Peter or I could ever had expected.

Over twenty years later Peter turned up at my house one Sunday afternoon. He was on one of his nostalgia trips. 'Let's nip round and see Ted and Sybil and have a cup of tea,' he said. I told Audrey, my wife, we'd be back soon and off we drove. At Winchmore Hill, right near the golf course, handy for Ted's passion for the game, his wife Sybil opened the front door and nearly fainted. We hadn't seen her, or Ted, for many years. Peter at once put his fingers to his lips as we wanted to surprise Ted who we could hear was upstairs. They had a little padded bench seat in the hall and Peter and I sat on it, side by side like Tweedledum and Tweedledee and, to Sybil's amazement, without speaking a word, we both took our handkerchiefs out and tucked them under our chins. Ted kept calling out to Sybil wanting to know who was at the front door. Eventually, he had to come downstairs to see. We both sat, like naughty schoolboys, waiting for him to laugh like he'd done before, but Ted fooled us. Halfway down the stairs he saw us, stopped, and Peter and I, embarrassed, saw tears running down his cheeks. I guess, in that moment, he'd realized our journey was a tribute from us, to him, in memory of those happy times. Oh, he was a lovely man.

* * *

Both Pete and I got through a lot of radio work in those days (much of it together), and we managed to earn a reasonable living. The Beeb, as the BBC is still affectionately known, paid you in that wonderfully archaic denomination known as the guinea (one pound, one shilling). They also had a monopoly, and well they knew it. Work on radio, become a household name, then cash in via the commercial theatre. That was the name of the game. My first broadcasts were at a fee of four guineas and it took me three years to get it raised to six. But who cared. Peter and I rushed from studio to studio playing as many characters as the script writers demanded. We were either enjoying Life With The Lyons, Meeting The Huggetts or Educating Archie. Then came the Film.

Early in 1952, in a basement room in Wardour Street, we were redubbing film reels of Laurel and Hardy. A bright gentleman had bought some cheap footage of Stan and Ollie, obviously intending to put out a little film of them. I imagine it was cheap as it was soon discovered there was no sound track and he had to employ two actors to put voices on the film. Peter was booked as Hardy, he suggested me as Laurel. All day long we sat watching loops of film being projected on the screen and gradually began to realize just how ahead of their time those two marvellous comics were. I just know Peter always adored them and I think he was very influenced by their subtlety. But it was frustrating just to voice a film; if only we could be up there on the silver screen. However, our good fairy was at hand in the person of Jimmy Grafton.

Jimmy Grafton was one of those wonderful stage-struck people show business owes so much to. The Grafton Arms in Victoria was the public house owned by his family, and he ran it with great style, but his real passion was the world of entertainment. Until his death he managed the career of Harry Secombe, he wrote scripts, and he ran a theatrical agency on the side, but, undoubtedly, he will go down in theatrical history as the person who, to a great extent, was responsible for setting up what was soon to be an explosion in the world of British comedy, namely *The Goon Show*.

Through my friendship with Pete I was taken one night to the Grafton Arms, one of those wonderful Victorian pubs, all etched glass partitions, and gilt-embellished plasterwork. Just to the left entrance (I can see it now) was an upright piano at which sat a shabby, raincoated, gaunt figure playing rather better jazz than you would expect to find in a public house. Peter pointed at the figure. 'That', he said, rather proudly, 'is Milligan.' His introduction made me aware that here was someone of some importance, and later I found out in what affection Pete held Spike Milligan. An affection that see-sawed with fury, exasperation and, to a certain extent, envy.

I'd heard plenty of rumours about Spike and found most of them to be true. Unstable, and yet highly professional. Gullible, and yet cunning. A complex about his lack of education, but so talented as to be frightening. A natural musician, able to play almost any instrument handed to him, he suffered the constant torture of frustration that always seems to accompany people with natural artistic talent. He was also one of the best comic writers of his time. By corralling Peter, Harry Secombe, Michael Bentine and Spike together Jimmy sowed the seeds of a radio show *Crazy People*. This really appalling title, with its zany 'Let's all have fun around the mircrophone' tone, soon gave way, fortunately, to the title of the show that is still spoken of with awe in comedy circles. To this day recordings are played, world-wide, of the series which was to influence Peter for the rest of his life.

Using sound effects as they had never been used before, and digging deep into the great tradition of surrealist English eccentric humour, exemplified by Edward Lear and Lewis Carroll, *The Goon Show* was sound anarchy. Without rhyme or reason, the characters Peter, Harry, Michael and Spike played peopled a mythical kingdom equivalent to a comic Gormenghast. Still in its early days and before it quite reached the cult status it would soon do, the show was already creating enough stir to convince yet another entrepreneur, E. J. Fancy, that there was money to be made out of a film featuring them. In April, 1952, in a small studio in Maida Vale, Peter, Spike, Harry, and Bentine starred in an epic production called *Down Among the Z Men*. I was there in a smaller capacity as a baddie.

The first morning of filming, Peter and I learnt a lesson which we never forgot. Full of excitement and enthusiasm, we cornered the poor, innocent director as he was surveying the tiny set, no doubt wondering how, in God's name, he was going to shoot in this cramped area, and what was he doing trying to get a picture out in two weeks with an inexperienced cast. To add salt to the wound he was then faced with two actors, one dressed as a military man (Peter) the other as a crook (me). Peter started by launching into his own personal exposition of his part. 'I feel,' he said, 'that the character I am playing has certain undercurrents of repression which I might best express by having a noticeable twitch.'

Then it was my turn. 'If I could just suggest the cigarette always stuck in the side of the mouth,' I said, 'thereby allowing me a permanent sneer, I think it might add considerably to the depth of my portrayal.'

The director, a tall figure, still wearing his RAF officer's greatcoat, gazed above our heads for a silent moment. Then he looked down at us. 'I've got eight minutes' screen time a day to shoot,' he said. 'Do it quickly.' He then walked away.

In the obscure world of early-morning or late-night TV, films like *Down Among the Z Men* still get shown and, sadly, they don't improve with age. It's interesting, however, to see Peter on film so early on. Obviously he didn't bother with the twitch (no cigarette for me either) but he did manage, even then, to play more realistically than the rest of us.

* * *

During this period I spent a lot of time with Pete at the Hyde Park flat and marvelled at the way Anne seemed to cope with the frantic scene going on all round her. And it was frantic. A pattern emerged that stayed with Peter all his life. If at all possible everything had to be brought round. His hair was cut at home, the new suit fitted in the living room, his comedy scripts spread across the dining room table. Most wives of actors have to be tolerant but Anne really was tolerant above and beyond the call of matrimony. On top of which she had to deal with my photography.

Every man dreams of discovering some wonderful aphrodisiac that will make his conquest of the lady he desires a dead certainty. In the RAF I knew an airman who bought some Spanish fly in Cairo which he carefully guarded until we got back to England. 'There's this darling in Ruislip,' he said. 'Always fancied her and I reckon this will do the trick.' He invited the innocent maiden round, slipped some of it in her tea, waited five minutes, then pounced. She walloped him round the ear with her handbag, stormed out of the house, and I gather he never saw her again.

Well, I can't say I went round slipping nasty brown powder in cups of tea but I did have my photography. I'd always been mad about it and now had an expensive camera, plus a fully fitted darkroom. To my delight, glamorous actresses, realizing my pictures were really quite good, trotted on their high heels to my flat and demurely posed. After all, every actress in our profession needs photographs. Peter cottoned on immediately and before you could say Friese Green he was down to Wallace Heaton's in Bond Street, the Rolls-Royce of camera dealers, and apparently bought every piece of equipment. The only problem was Pete didn't have the slightest idea how to use it. His friend Graham would oblige with a lesson so, one quiet Sunday, there we were, monopolizing the bathroom. The enlarger perched precariously on the linen basket, the developing dishes on a bit of plywood placed over the bath, and the safety light in place of the normal bulb.

Peter had managed to take a few pictures, which he'd had developed locally, and was desperate to see how they looked enlarged.

When we did gradually see the image appear in the developer I could see why. He'd persuaded a girlfriend of Anne's to pose for him. What is more he'd got her to pose in a bikini. Even with my experience of photography I'd never got that far with a girl. Peter could see I was impressed, but he was there to learn and conscientiously watched as we approached the final stage. An elementary technique after enlarging is a thing called 'touching up'. Any dust on the negative appears on the enlarged print as a white dot, and the technique for getting rid of it is to 'touch up' the print with a fine, sable brush, dipped in spotting medium.

Well, it was open war. There was the large print of the young lady, and there were Peter and I, viewing all the white dust spots on various parts of her anatomy. At once we got into an argument as to who was to touch up where. Like schoolboys we fought over the spheres of influence, each staking a claim to his favourite area. 'The breasts are definitely mine,' said Pete. 'You can concentrate on the bum.' Before things got too nasty there was a knock on the door; it was Anne, reminding Peter that he had a recording of *The Goon Show* to do that night and was due for rehearsal.

Peter was beside himself. 'Oh Christ, Gra,' he said, sable brush in hand. 'What are we going to do?' Then a look of inspiration. Up went the phone and Peter dialled the BBC. 'Put me through to Peter Eton [Producer of *The Goon Show*], he said, in a perfectly ordinary voice. A few seconds' pause, then suddenly the voice was a dreadful croaking gasp. 'Sorry to call like this Peter, but I just couldn't get through rehearsal. Laryngitis, it's killing me.' The gasping increased. 'But don't worry. I'll rest it and be there tonight. You know I'm a pro, I won't let you down.' The receiver went back on the rest. Pete, voice now normal, gave me a look. 'Maybe I'm being unfair. Perhaps you ought to have a go at the breasts, while I have a go at the bum.'

CHAPTER THREE

DAME GRAHAM STARK

At the same time as working so much with Peter I was also doing another radio series, *All Star Bill*, written by two comedy writers who, like Spike, became legends in their lifetimes. Ray Galton and Alan Simpson originally joined the show as a temporary stop gap as the original writers were a disaster. Both very tall, and very large, they had met in a TB ward of a hospital, heard a lot of radio while still in bed and, rightly convinced they could do as well, sent in a trial script. From reading the first page it was obvious they were in a class of their own, and Tony Hancock, myself and Moira Lister, the three resident performers, knew we had a potential hit. Tony was working better than ever, and Alan and Ray's material shot him higher and higher. He was still a friend, but gradually there seemed to be growing in him the hunger for absolute perfection that tragically brought him to despair and self-desctruction.

Another tormented performer was Spike Milligan. Cursed with intermittent attacks of acute depression which he, in his lucid moments, called the Black Doom, he was forced to get medical help and, every so often, go into a nursing home. *The Goon Show* still had to be recorded every Sunday and the producer, Peter Eton, hit on the idea of replacing Spike, temporarily, with two performers playing alternately; he chose Dick Emery and me. It gave me the chance to work yet again with Peter and be fascinated, once more, by his style. With uncanny instinct he seemed able to get the maximum laugh with the minimum effort. But he never really felt at ease dealing with an audience. Jovial Harry Secombe could go out in front of two thousand people and put them in his pocket in moments. He adored them, they adored him. Spike, the most unpredictable performer that ever walked on a stage, could nevertheless, on a good night, have a theatre helpless with laughter. Peter, however, spent some of the worst moments of his life having to face 'Them,' the term he bitterly used for the audience. What happened with him at Coventry Hippodrome has gone down in theatrical history.

Coventry Hippodrome was the great prestige theatre of the Midlands, and its owner was Sam Newsome. A born showman, Newsome protectively guarded the reputation of the Hippodrome as Val Parnell did the London Palladium. Everything had to be of the best: the sets, the costumes, the musicians. Like the captain of a great Atlantic liner Newsome prowled that theatre, constantly checking everything was running smoothly. Well, everything was until Peter played there.

The Goons were riding high. Everyone listened to the show on the radio, and it was only a question of time before large cheques were waved in their direction tempting them to play to a live audience. Harry was fine. With a singing voice guaranteed to shatter all hearing aids within forty feet, and a tried and tested comedy routine handy, he was a natural. Spike could ad lib better than anyone I ever saw and he also happened to play the trumpet rather brilliantly. Blow a few high Cs and he could walk off to a roar of applause. That left Peter. Tempted by the money, he made the disastrous mistake of playing Coventry, and it is still some sort of miracle that he lived to tell the tale.

The theatre was booked to capacity but from the word go it was death of a dog time for Pete. Twice nightly he walked on to the sound of his own footsteps, told his jokes, got absolutely no laughs, and twice nightly he walked off again to the same lonely noise. Then came the Wednesday matinée. Even Spike and Harry were finding it hard. Peter walked quietly on, carrying a chair and a wind-up gramophone. He looked at the audience. They looked at him. All two thousand of them. At the back of the pit Sam Newsome was keeping an eye on things. Then the orchestra stirred as all orchestras will when the routine is changed. Peter had never brought on a chair before, and certainly not a wind-up gramophone. He didn't tell any jokes. He just put his foot up on the chair, balanced the gramophone on his knee, wound it up and then, in a cultivated voice said 'I am well aware that there are many music lovers amongst you today.' The orchestra's jaws dropped and the audience became even quieter. 'Therefore,' continued Peter, producing a record, 'I have brought this lovely recording, by my friend Walter Stott and his orchestra, of "Silent Night", and I intend to play it for you.' And he did. All the way through.

As the last notes died he bowed, closed the gramophone, picked up the chair, and walked off. There was total and absolute silence from the audience, but not from Sam Newsome. He gave a roar and it was only the fact that the fire door, between the stage and the auditorium, was locked that saved Peter from certain death.

About this time, over in Hollywood, the movie moguls were gearing themselves up to fight the growing menace, to them, of television. As aerial after aerial sprouted skyward they mounted wide screen epics that would dwarf the small flickering screen. It was the start of the giant historical epics that made the fortunes of leading men with the legs, torsos and biceps suitable for wearing Roman centurion costumes. Unfortunately for

Hollywood, the establishment of England was about to mount an equally lavish production that would dwarf those monster stucco sets that were going up on the back lots of the studios of Los Angeles.

The King was dead, long live the Queen. The Coronation of Elizabeth II brought an audience to those small, black and white, flickering screens that altered, for ever, the whole pattern of entertainment in the British Isles. TV was joked about but came the day, and office staffs were depleted, television set owners were suddenly the social darlings, and several million viewers could view, close up, live, and free, a romantic pageant that made them realize you really could have your cake and eat it by merely sitting in front of that box.

Showbiz leapt on the band wagon and one of my proudest possessions is my original script, dated 1 June 1953.

This show was recorded at the Playhouse Theatre, then a BBC outside recording studio. As far as I know it's the only copy of the script in existence. Spike admitted this to me after the sale of his *Goon Show* scripts some years ago to Elton John. Who knows, if Elton reads this, he might take an offer. But I'm afraid I'd have to turn it down. If there are a few occasions in your professional life that you think of as a highlight, that was one of mine.

In our private life Peter and I continued our

relationship, which at this time, was centred on our shared delight in making models (and I'm talking about plastic kits you got in boxes), photography, and writing funny letters to each other. I once sent him a letter, purporting to come from George C. Blinks, market research expert, telling him he'd been selected to receive a plastic kit which, when assembled, would make a life-sized human being, the sex of which could be determined by the person making up the model. Mr Blinks even hinted that a small battery-operated motor was in the pipeline which would animate said model. The letter must have been one of my better efforts as Pete rang up, very excited, to tell me he was about to receive this quite remarkable kit. 'Just think what we can do with it,' he said. 'Especially when we get the motor going!' It was obvious Peter had plans to make the female version and I'm afraid the mental picture of him carefully and painstakingly assembling a full, motorized, plastic, female body gave me the giggles and him the realization I'd written the letter. He joined in the fun but his laugh didn't really cover the disappointment.

When the mood took me I would also write to him under the *nom de plume* of Colonel 'Mad Jack' Stark, who was based in the fictitious Secunderabad Villas in Brixton. The letters were peopled with ludicrous characters such as Boadicea Nungwhitely, spinster of this parish;

Erica Ploon, barmaid of the local pub, the Dutch Cap and Bells; Ali Ben Higgins, who ran the local fish and chip shop, and, finally, Mr Eric Moboto, foreman of the local protective teat factory. It even got to the stage that I actually physically re-created one character I invented, a certain Marcel Cassette, who was a 1920s idiotic Frenchman, much addicted to bicycle racing and 'le tennis'. I took a self-portrait of Marcel and made sure Peter got a print.

Peter wrote in return under three aliases. There was Herr Piece, a Teutonic gentleman based in Wicn In Der Bedd. When in Los Angeles, Pete would invariably write from the desk of Rex Finchley, MD of Sub-Human Artists Inc. Finally, Major Bludnuk, Retd, late of Her Majesty's 41st Mounted Deserters, would drop me a line. They were ridiculous letters, and pictures, but such a lot of fun, and we did enjoy ourselves.

My letters were always addressed to Major Dennis Bludnuk c/o Peter Sellers. Bludnuk was a character invented by Spike in the *Goon Show* and Peter soon seized upon it, fleshing it out, having recognised that Spike had created something as immortal as Micawber. A congenital coward, and epitome of the British Raj, Bludnuk always remained a favourite character of Peter's and he re-created a sophisticated version of him years later in a cameo performance in the film *The Wrong Box*, directed by Bryan Forbes, and starring Michael Caine and the *Who's Who* of British cinema actors. In the picture Peter played Dr Pratt, an inebriated locum surrounded by a horde of mangy cats. I wasn't the only one who thought that it was a consummate performance which could easily rank with some of the best things Peter ever did.

In the summer of 1984, one of the great passions of my young cinema days came to London to star in the play *Aren't We All* at the Haymarket Theatre opposite Rex Harrison. Just writing the name Claudette Colbert conjures up her ravishing smile, and in real life she was just as delightful. Through my friendship with Francis Matthews, who was appearing at the Haymarket with her, I met her backstage. Possibly I hoped for magical stories of pre-war Hollywood but our entire conversation centered on the amazing performance Peter gave as Dr Pratt. She was obviously a fan of everything he'd done but selected that single sequence as one of the highlights of his career.

To understand what set Peter apart you only have to see him, at the end of the scene, after playing some wonderful comedy, lean forward so he is nose to nose with one of the cats and utter his final line, 'It doesn't do you any good, you know.' The line, in itself, means nothing but, in the context of the scene, and spoken with such sadness, it implied so much. Guilt, sorrow, failure. I once found out from Bryan Forbes that Peter had put the line in as an ad lib, and Bryan had the good taste to leave it in the film.

Instinct governed Peter's work to a great extent. Maddening to directors, and other performers, he would suddenly switch a line, or insert some dialogue and, even under pressure, wouldn't change his mind. Assailed by somebody for making an unscripted change, the chin would lift ever so slightly, the eyes would narrow as he looked at the objector, and God help you if you didn't heed the warning signs. Stick out for what you wanted and hell could break loose. First would come the sarcasm suggesting you were obviously some sort of simpleton, and that really you would be better employed elsewhere as deciding on standards of comedy was obviously not your métier. If you decided to stand your ground Peter could walk off a film set quicker than you could say 'but we have a contract'. Alongside his disregard for social position or status, Pete regarded contracts as something lawyers and business men drew up in obscure offices that were to be ignored if they got in the way of creating a performance. Hell for producers, but amazing when you saw the final result.

I often disapproved of things Peter got up to

as an actor, especially when he used his status as a lever, but when it came to him not caring for power and social position then he was my boy. Hypocrisy and the game of fawning were not in his book. To use a lovely English phrase he never gave a bugger. Naturally, a fund of stories of Peter's battles became part and parcel of the backstage gossips' repertoire. During rehearsals of a television show I was once doing with Warren Mitchell, Peter was being discussed. By this time he was a huge international star, but the story being told, with malicious relish by a producer, of Peter's famous remarks about the then head of Comedy at the BBC, Tom Sloane, dated back to Pete's early TV days.

Peter had done a live TV show (not much of a success), and during it he'd leapt in front of the camera and declaimed that it was all the fault of Tom Sloane and his blasted liniment. Every executive at the BBC that night nearly had a coronary. Peter had not only attacked a head of a department, he'd also mentioned a well known commercial product. And all on live TV! The long story ended. The producer gave a knowing smirk. 'My God, everybody was *so* furious!' he said. There was the slightest pause, then Warren raised his head. 'I know,' he said. 'Did Peter's career a lot of harm!'

They say to laugh is to stay young. Whenever we got together Pete and I seemed to be perpetual schoolboys. Riots of laughter brought about by the most unlikely things. Instruction books—not you would have thought a great mine for comedy—constantly delighted us. It started with my first typewriter, an elegant electric model made by Olivetti. Perhaps the Italian parentage of this machine affected the prose in the accompanying booklet. It gave the conventional instructions then, like a bolt out of the blue, when discussing the actual use of the keyboard, it told you to 'strike home smartly'. Peter found a beauty in the final paragraph of the book that came with his Volkswagen (naturally he owned one of those as he changed his car, on average, weekly). After reams of technical data it ended with a terse, but telling Teutonic statement. 'By owning this car,' it said, 'think of the money you save.'

Well, we agreed on the instruction book jokes but when it came to obeying them, that was a different matter. At this stage I must admit that I'm the sort of person that has to answer the phone if it rings. At airports I instantly obey commands that issue from the public address system, and as for instruction books . . . 'Under no circumstances remove panel D!' They don't tell you why, but I never argue. I'd rather be broken on the wheel than remove panel D. Not Pete. He'd remove panel D at the drop of a screwdriver and even if he was told not to rotate knurled knob Y without first making sure that extension arm P was fully inserted he'd just ignore it. Peter worked on the simple principle that gadgets were fun and designed to make his life easy, and not the other way round. We also differed on packaging. I've always suffered from a dread disease called openingtheboxitis. Show me a lovely piece of packaging and it's on with the surgical gloves, out with the Stanley knife, and the operation begins. A delicate incision through the cellophane, a careful prising apart of those beautiful polystyrene casings, carefully revealing the object, usually camera equipment, that I've bought. Pete believed in brute force. He'd tear the box open, ignore the instruction book, and press every button until something worked.

It was just the same with cars. Unlock the door, key in ignition, select gear, accelerate and away. Heaven help the dealer if anything went wrong. Peter somehow saw me as a co-test driver, and with every new car I became the first passenger. He was never satisfied until I had given it full approval. It was a new Jaguar that nearly put paid to this relationship. A terrible squeak from the rear of the car drove Peter mad. 'Gra, we've got to find it,' he said. As I knew that if we didn't it would be straight back to the garage with a demand for the return of his money, I felt I should do the decent thing and try to help. All over the rear of that car I clambered while Pete drove. On the floor, on the seat, ear pressed to the rear parcel shelf, but no luck. The squeak was louder but nothing you could pin-point. We pulled up and Peter went into his final appeal. He felt that as a fellow lover of fine machinery, a connoisseur of quality merchandise, *and* his closest personal friend, he was justified in asking me for the supreme sacrifice. Would I ride in the boot of the car while he, ever so carefully and slowly, drove no more than a few hundred feet?

In a moment of weakness I agreed, and gingerly climbed into the capacious boot, carefully holding up the lid by a few inches. Ever so carefully and slowly did my friend drive, but neither he nor I reckoned on the sod's law factor, namely the young moron in the sports car who cut Peter up very savagely. Reflex actions are hard to control and Peter put his foot down and off we went. The lid slammed shut, I bounced up and down in the darkness, while carbon monoxide filled the cramped space at an alarming rate. Fortunately the next lights were red and Peter had to pull up. Realizing now what an idiot he'd been he shot out of the car, ran round to the boot and opened it, just as a lady driver pulled up behind the Jaguar. She saw me climbing, coughing hard, out of the boot and, convinced she was watching an acolyte of the Kray twins doing his bit for the firm put her car in reverse and shot back down the road.

*   *   *

Nineteen-fifty-four was the year I did my first summer show in Cromer, a seaside resort on the north coast of Norfolk. Lovely place, lovely show, and Cromer crabs are the best seafood I've ever eaten. Even more than pantomime the summer show can be one of the most enjoyable types of entertainment to be in (especially at children's matinées), and it is one of the greatest training grounds in the world for a comic. A diminutive assistant stage manager, who dementedly rushed about backstage helping with the props, was also being permitted to perform for the first time as a comic. Terrified, he went on the first night, did six minutes, and died like a dog. He shouted every joke and mistimed most of his material. He was very close to tears in the wings, and red-faced with shame. I told him not to worry. 'With your charm, which I wish I had, all you've got to do is relax and you can't miss.' He thanked me, did just that, and Ronnie Corbett never looked back.

At the end of the three-month season I was awarded the Bucket and Spade Oscar for being the best comic in Summer Show (the award should have gone to the producer, Clive Dunn, who showed me every trick of the trade). There was a publicity shot taken and there stands

Peter in the background. He'd not only volunteered to be in the picture, he even agreed to wear a terrible pierrot hat as well, and that's what I call friendship.

That winter I was initiated into playing the variety theatres round the provinces, returning to London every Sunday to appear in the radio show *Educating Archie*. By this time Peter and Spike were living in the same block of flats in Highgate and it was a case of killing two birds with one stone when I went to call. Well, not so much killing two birds—more like deciding which flat to have dinner in. Spike's wife, June, and Peter's wife, Anne, were both splendid cooks and I did get spoiled for choice. I always was a bit on the thin side and perhaps they both thought I needed fattening up. Nothing like being a skinny bachelor for bringing out the maternal instinct in women.

At the start of 1956 I did a television show with Richard Hearne. He'd made a big hit as a character called Mr Pastry, and on the strength of that had his own series. The show featured a pirate sketch in which lots of cardboard cutlasses were waved about. Dickie Hearne, as the comic ship's cook, whirled a long string of sausages round his head, trying to fight off a boarding party of wicked pirates, who were led by myself as the chief villain. Highly sophisticated entertainment, but it was a lot of fun. The wardrobe department had a field day with my appearance. A black patch over one eye, a shiny steel hook sprouting from my sleeve and, just so nobody would have any doubts about my being a pirate, a wooden leg. Considering I had to keep my head cocked to one side so I could see properly, avoid stabbing my fellow actors to death with that hook, and make sure the wooden leg didn't get stuck in a knot hole in the deck, I think I managed to get through the scene reasonably well.

I got a call from Peter the next morning. 'Saw you on the TV last night,' he said. 'I noticed how you dealt with the eye patch, and that bleeding hook, and with having your leg tied up behind you. How much would you like to do the *Goon Show* television series?' An actor fighting against odds was just the thing to appeal to Peter's sense of humour, and I always silently thank that over-zealous wardrobe department for starting me off into a new area of television.

Idiots Weekly, Price Tuppence, written with the extraordinary invention that Spike Milligan possessed, was the title of the series (later changed to *A Show Called Fred*), first shown on 24 February 1956, and from the word go it became a cult. Groups of addicts gathered in front of TV sets and marvelled at just what Peter and Spike were doing. Overnight they changed British television comedy. Up to then it was glittering night club sets in which elegant gentlemen, in white tie and tails, told oh-so-terribly upper-class jokes. They alternated with jovial fat men, usually doing a knees-up in a saloon bar, wearing flat caps and holding sticks of Blackpool rock, which equally fat woman pointed at, screaming, 'Ooh, ain't you got a big one!'

Then *Idiots Weekly* came along from which stemmed the whole new approach to the English comedy. To this day the entire *Monty Python* ensemble pay homage to the show and admit it influenced and shaped their approach to comedy, while in America Mel Brooks and Woody Allen speak of that visual and verbal *Goon* humour with reverence. To its eternal credit commercial television, in those early days not too well known for its vision in the world of entertainment (after all, it had been created to act as a vendor), had given Peter and Spike carte blanche. It had also given us a young Canadian director, Dick Lester, who had the good sense to realize that he had to tread the fine line between lunatic invention and coherence.

Spike was in his element as he discovered the magic world of TV. From the start he was never content to let the camera be an impersonal piece of glass, merely a porthole for the viewer to look through. His visual inventiveness never seemed to slacken and, in Peter, he had the perfect performer to work with. No attitude of 'well,

I've got to put in my funny walk here', or 'I don't think I ought to be seen doing that'. There were no reservations, and Peter and Spike had assembled a cast that went along with them all the way. But how could we object? Here was the show that every comedy actor had dreamt of, but never thought would come to fruition. We broke all the rules but we were also a palpable hit.

To re-create in words visual comedy is a dreadful risk but a risk one has to take if only to stress the extraordinary chances that Peter, as a performer, took in those shows. And it was infectious. Ken Connor, Valentine Dyall, Patti Lewis, myself, all of us accepted whatever we were asked to do. In one of Spike's more joyous sequences we played out-of-work actors making a living by deputizing for animals at the zoo, which entailed Ken Connor going in a cage with monkeys, Valentine Dyall joining a vulture in its cage, and myself swimming, clad only in a bathing costume, in the sea lion pit—with the sea lions. When the film was played back in the studio later I saw Peter actually cry with laughter while he watched the vulture nervously edge away along a branch as Val Dyall climbed in with it.

In the middle of a certain sketch one camera suddenly took a wide shot of the studio, showing all the rest of the cameras, as well as the cast. Then the studio doors swung open and three other cameras burst in, all labelled BBC. The cameramen on those cameras were wearing plumed hats and announced they were the BBC Light Cavalry cameras, come to steal a free show. Our cameramen immediately drew wooden swords and battle commenced. It was glorious anarchy.

Without a doubt the high spot of a series which seemed to be filled with glorious set pieces, was Peter's impression of Laurence Olivier's Richard III. Actually, that description is wrong. It was beyond an impression. It was Peter, using the look, the face, and the voice of Olivier to give a marvellous reading of the part. The Shakespearian pastiche was a glorious send-up of the Olivier film and, for the obvious reason, everyone wondered what 'you know who' would think of it. Spike thought up a wonderful joke ending. After the sketch was over he wanted to see a long shot of a lone spear carrier on the battlements. The figure would not have moved throughout. Finally the camera would track slowly forward to a close shot of the figure, then the visor would be raised and we would see Olivier himself. A pause then, with a resigned look, he would slowly shake his head. But how could anyone suggest such a thing to that godlike actor, then at the height of his fame? We found out later that Olivier was a great fan of the show and, told of the suggested ending, said, 'If only they'd asked me.'

CHAPTER FOUR

RICHARD THE THIRD GOES WEST

The grapevine of show business spread the news of this extraordinary show even overseas and, near the end of the year, Peter and I were booked to go to Toronto to play the Richard the Third sketch for the prestigious Chrysler Show on CBC Television in Toronto, which was to be networked to the USA. I was going with Peter as I played the other major role, the Duke of Clarence. As it turned out, I travelled in advance as CBC needed someone to explain all the intricate working of the props. Peter couldn't get there until the night before the show so CBC generously arranged for me to go via New York, where I spent the weekend with Julie Andrews and her then husband, Tony Walton. I'd been friends with Julie for many years and she was delighted to have someone from London come and visit. It was arranged for me to stay at the Park Chambers where she and Tony were living. Even more important, for the night I arrived, Saturday, she saw to it I had the 'house seats' for *My Fair Lady* in which she and Rex Harrison were starring. By that time they were literally the King and Queen of Broadway as their show was the biggest smash hit the Great White Way had ever known.

The cab driver who drove me to the Mark Hellinger Theatre that night was furious. 'How come you get to see *My Fair Lady*, huh? You bein' a limey and just orf the plane. Me, I been tryin to see it for t'ree years!' His name was Herbie Horowitz. I know that because all New York taxi drivers are called Herbie Horowitz. When I told him Julie had personally given me the seats then things changed. If there's one thing a New York cab driver likes it's fame, and the fact that I was a friend of Julie's was enough for Herbie. When we got to the theatre he uttered words that I had never heard from a cab driver before or, for that matter, since. 'You ain't payin',' he said. 'She's a sweet lady and, bein' a friend of hers, you gotta be a nice guy, so hands across the sea and all that sort of thing, old sport.' He gave a grin and drove off.

Tuesday morning I flew to Toronto and was given my first example of New World know-how and liked it. The director and I walked the set and I explained how certain things had to be changed. I looked at a small mattress at the back of the set. 'Got to be bigger than that,' I said. 'I have to fall on it.' The fingers snapped and almost at once three double-bed mattresses were piled one on top of the other. I pointed to a clock they'd carefully built. Apologetically, in my best British tentative manner, I told him it might just be ever so slightly too small. The fingers snapped once more. 'Rebuild it,' he said. Even as we turned away it was being pulled off the wall.

Peter arrived the next day and was just as impressed, but in his eyes I could see signs of mounting fear. Normally I never knew Peter to have stage fright, he just went on and did it, but here we were, for the first time, exporting a brand of comedy that was revolutionary even for a country as renowned for its eccentric humour as Britain. During the day, large, well-dressed, cigar-toting Chrysler executives nervously prowled behind the cameras, watching every move we made as Pete and I mechanically went through the paces of the sketch. Without the stimulus of an audience comedy actors are nothing. Desperately trying to bolster their own egos (after all, they had flown Peter and me to Toronto), the executives anxiously scanned every face for signs that their decision had been right. And there were some faces to scan. Seated in the stalls (the show was being recorded at a huge cinema called Loews Uptown) was the rest of the cast. The Italian opera star, Tito Gobbi. Larry Adler, the most famous harmonica player in the world. Percy Faith and his forty-piece orchestra, plus the actor Hume Cronyn, who was compering the show. Then there was Celeste Holm, a lady who had held her own with Bette Davis in *All About Eve*, and was later to do the same thing with

Frank Sinatra in *High Society*, singing 'Who Wants To Be A Millionaire?'. Each and every one of them sat with that sympathetic air that performers always give their fellow artistes, but there wasn't a smile to be seen.

Pete and I shared a dressing room, and a few hours later he looked at himself in a mirror. He was fully dressed, hump and all, as Richard III. The wig and make-up finalizing the extraordinary transformation. There was a moment's silence, then, in that perfect Olivier voice, he said, 'Now is the winter of an absolute bleeding disaster!' I moved up behind his shoulder until he could see me reflected in the mirror. 'Watch my lips,' I said and carefully mouthed Golden Bollocks. He took one look at me as I stood there, trying hard to look dignified, dressed up to the nines as the Duke of Clarence, wearing flowing robes and a rather fetching blond wig, and burst into laughter. The smell of fear evaporated and on the set we went. As the floor manager gave the cue, Peter silently limped towards the camera, started the famous soliloquy, and we were a smash. Every joke got its laugh, every bit of visual comedy the right reaction. The Chrysler boys were over the moon. One gave me a slap on the back. 'Oh God, I love it, I love it!' he said. He was about to slap Peter on the back then looked at the hump and changed his mind. Celeste Holm, hanging on to a piece of scenery and dabbing at her mascara with a paper tissue, gave us the best compliment of the night. 'You're twenty years ahead of us,' she said.

Pete and I flew back to New York, this time lying back in our seats instead of sitting on the edge of them. After years of exposure to American show business via the movies, radio, and now television, we had an inferiority complex about the quality and expertise of American show business that was hard to shake off, but we'd done and dared. Here was a classic example of taking a gamble, which was the name of Peter's game, by performing something so totally British in style and eccentricity, instead of mistakenly going into that boring mid-Atlantic no man's land. And the Americans had loved it. I think that single show, more than any other, made Peter realize that the bastion of America could be stormed although, paradoxically, he was never that interested. In reality he never really liked America, or the Americans. He would make exceptions with Europeanized ones like Stanley Kubrick but by and large he seemed actively to dislike them and often would go out of his way to antagonize them. They say one can usually trace aversion back to some simple word or action but I never did find out just what it was that made him so anti-American.

I was the exact reverse. I liked the speed with which they got things done, and I liked the democracy that existed on their films and TV shows. Their love of success was a bit overpowering but at least they never had that deep distrust of talent that the majority of people in Britain appeared to have. It always seemed sad to me that, with the best actors in the world, the British still ranked them slightly below bookmakers when it came to the social scale. It was the total reverse in America, where to be an actor was to be Class with a capital C. As soon as Reagan ran for President I knew he was a dead cert to win. One thing Pete did like about America was the way they adored the British accent. Particularly the women. In no time at all we were talking with voices reminiscent of pre-war Wodehouse upper-class twits. In New York we only had two days to do the sights and shops. Maggie Smith and I went shopping for ladies' underwear together. She was working in New York at the time and, knowing I wanted something special for a girlfriend of mine in London, she gallantly helped a fellow Brit out by braving the crush at Bloomingdales' lingerie counter. Bad enough to discuss brassieres and knickers at Marks and Spencer's. I was damned if I was going to do it in America.

* * *

Back in England, on the historic date of 2 March 1958, Peter, Spike, Harry and I went off to Cambridge University solemnly playing tiddlywinks on behalf of the Duke of Edinburgh and the National Playing Fields Association. It seems that an unchivalrous slur was cast upon the Duke when a Cambridge University magazine suggested he might be a cheat at tiddlywinks. Immediately, for reasons that were never quite clear, we were appointed his champions and, determined to avenge the Royal honour, went off to Cambridge and were beaten 120 to 50. In the telegram he sent in support, Prince Philip assured us he would have been there in person but sadly, while practising, he had pulled a muscle in his winking finger. I've still got the tie, woven exclusively for the members of our small team, which bears the emblem of a rampant tiddle.

* * *

Another historic date in 1958 was the 16th of October. Peter called inviting me to join him at the opening night of Judy Garland at the Dominion. 'I've got two tickets, but Anne doesn't fancy going.' I knew Anne was heavily pregnant so I understood. When you went out with Pete you always went in style and, wearing black tie, we glided up to the theatre in a large, black, limousine. The show was sensational. The comic, Alan King, unknown to most of the audience, was a big hit, and Garland, if possible, was even better than when I first saw her at the London Palladium. Back in the car, going home, I remarked to Peter what a shame it was Anne couldn't go to the show. 'I know,' said Pete. 'But she would have found it a bit difficult.' What he didn't tell me was that she would have found it absolutely impossible. Peter had booked Anne into the London Clinic that evening and, while he and I were in the Dominion watching Judy Garland, she was giving birth to Peter's first daughter, Sarah.

Nowadays it seems heartless not to be present at your child's birth but in those days men were required not to be around at such times. My own wife, when our first baby was about to be born, begged my agent to see I had a job somewhere that would keep me away from the clinic. 'I just want to get on with it,' she said. 'Can't have him fainting all over the place.'

Peter was very much in love with Anne and, in fact, always stayed in love with her. She was a very good influence on him. Being an actress herself she really understood how he was always trying to go that little bit further with his comedy. Unfortunately for her, Peter's mother Peg was steadily chipping away at the marriage and, like some wicked fairy-tale witch, was for ever stirring her black cauldron, making sure her son was getting his fair share of spells cast over him. Anne had a very bad time where Peg was concerned, and even after the new baby was born Peg never declared any truce in the war against her.

The lengths to which Peg was prepared to go was epitomized by The Joint Christmas, and joint had nothing to do with meat or smoking a dodgy kind of cigarette. Peg's hatred of Anne extended to her parents, which ruled out, as far as Peg was concerned, any social contact with them whatsoever. Even at Christmas time, the season of goodwill and reunion, no truce was permitted in the vendetta, and a farcical situation, that even Alan Ayckbourn might have thought too complicated to use, took place. Every year, without fail, Peter and the two children, plus Anne and her parents, would have their Christmas dinner at lunchtime. Turkey eaten, crackers pulled, presents exchanged, funny hats worn. By five in the evening Anne's parents would say goodbye to their grandchildren and leave. A short while later Peg and Bill would arrive and the whole thing would be repeated. Turkey eaten, crackers pulled, presents exchanged, funny hats worn. This almost unbelievable set piece continued, year after year.

★ ★ ★

Of all the gadgets Peter loved, cars had to take first place. Focusing lenses and pressing release buttons on cameras were ecstasy to me. Double declutching and doing nought to sixty in ten seconds in any make of car were ecstasy to Pete. He once spent a fortune buying a Bentley chassis, then had a special body built on it and thus became the first owner of what became a classic car, the Bentley Continental. It had a one-off colour, which was deep maroon, with white leather upholstery inside. I got the first ride in it with him and we stopped traffic wherever we went. Later that day I got a frantic phone call. 'Christ, Gra, what am I going to do?' Such a plea for help has to be heeded. Round to the house I went, to see the magnificent Bentley neatly backed into the garage. There was one small problem. At least three feet of the bonnet still stuck out onto the driveway. Peter had forgotten to measure it.

Down the entire garage had to come, and a new one built. The day it was finished he was able to put the beautiful Bentley away safely. A work bench was built at the end of the new garage on which he put a half-gallon tin of the special paint, fourteen coats of which had been hand sprayed on the gleaming body. His son, Michael, aged four, then asked what the paint was for. Being honest Peter patiently explained it was touch-up paint. 'You see, Michael,' he said, 'if a stone shoots up from the road and damages the car, this paint goes on and covers up the marks.'

When Pete called the next day he didn't even speak, he just made terrible moaning noises. Finally I managed to decipher a few words and discovered that little Michael, worried that his father's lovely car might be damaged by those naughty stones, had got out of bed early, opened the half-gallon of paint and, with a large brush, had painted it all over the body. Luckily Anne came down first, saw what Michael had done, climbed in her Mini, still wearing her nightdress and dressing gown, pulled Michael in after her and, with a basic intuition of a mother protecting her young, drove into the countryside where she stayed with Michael for the rest of the day. On being told the news, the coach builders came at dawn, wrapped the car in a tarpaulin, put it on a trailer, and took it away so no one could see what damage had been done to that beautiful car.

* * *

Whoever designed the opening of a corned beef tin should, in my opinion, be given a medal. Not for efficiency. Far from it. But had I not cut my hand rather badly in trying to turn one of those awful keys I wouldn't have thrown the tin in the waste bin, got in my car, and gone to have supper in Gerry's Club in Shaftesbury Avenue. My brave attempt to eat with my left hand, while holding the bandaged right hand aloft to staunch the blood, caught the sympathetic eye of a beautiful actress, Audrey Nicholson. I'd already seen her in the revue she was currently appearing in and, turning my disability to advantage, struck up conversation. Three weeks later we were engaged.

* * *

There's quite a large field just by a major roundabout at the end of Totteridge Lane in north London where, one sunny Sunday morning in the middle of 1959, you might have seen a strange figure, dressed in Victorian knickerbockers, on his head a deerstalker, peering at a camera several hundred yards in front of him. By the camera a portly figure was beckoning with his forefinger. Gradually the figure in the knickerbockers, lured on by the beckoning finger, came closer and closer to the camera, finally peering, questioningly, into the lens. At that moment the other hand of the man, with a boxing glove on it, shot into the picture and knocked knickerbockers, deerstalker and all, flat on his back. The beckoning finger belonged to Leo McKern, and the lad wearing the knickerbockers was me. We were both helping to make a bit of cinema history by appearing in *The Running, Jumping, and Standing Still Film*.

It was so typical of Peter to organize this

miniature epic. He'd already made a big success in British films with *The Ladykillers, The Smallest Show on Earth, The Mouse That Roared* and several others but it was never his way to rest on his laurels. He still liked to take chances and he made no secret of his dislike of the fellow film actors, whom he called the Pinewood Ponces, who didn't. In their turn they couldn't stand Peter, who'd come into their midst with apparently no qualifications as an actor and yet had managed to get notices from the critics that each and every one of them would have, almost, given up his place in the queue for a possible future Oscar.

The Running, Jumping and Standing Still Film was only a short, made in black and white, and stood about as much chance of a cinema release as an early Bioscope, circa 1895. That is, had it been made by anyone else but Peter. Frenetically, Spike, Peter, Audrey, myself, Leo McKern, and any other passing actor we could find, ran about that field under the direction of Dick Lester, and from the moment the picture was finished it was a winner. Cinemas which had never played a short in their lives before booked it. Film societies fought to get copies, and finally it became a cult movie playing the giant American campus circuit. In its way it became the most imitated short comedy film of its kind and launched Dick Lester on a big career as a film director. Old Golden B had done it again.

But he deserved it. Always had to take a chance had our Pete. Unfortunately, by doing so, the list of people he rubbed up the wrong way grew at an alarming rate. At least, however, he was consistent: once an enemy, always an enemy. One day I was at Peter's flat in Hampstead, and we were in the middle of one of our tinkering with gadgets afternoons, when the phone went. I was much too involved with either rotating knob B, or checking that I wasn't interfering with extension arm Y, to take a lot of notice of what Peter was talking about. However, I was aware that he was making lots of those flat Hmmn noises which I knew from experience meant the undercurrent of annoyance was getting a bit near the surface. Finally the phone went down and he was back, peering at the equipment we were trying to make work, when he suddenly looked at me. 'You know who that was, don't you?' he said. As I was in the middle of a delicate bit of soldering I couldn't start getting into a guessing game so I made a non-committal grunt. 'Only Harold Bloody Fielding,' he said. I must admit this piece of information did make me raise my head. Harold Bloody Fielding was one of the major impresarios of England and had mounted, and was still to mount, some of the most extravagant and successful musical shows ever seen in the country. A force to be reckoned with.

'Ah,' I said, rather cautiously, as I knew Harold Fielding had produced the first summer show Peter had ever appeared in at Southsea and, I gathered, their relationship had not been of the best. In fact Peter had told me that Fielding's parting words to him had been the old theatrical cliché, 'I'll see you never work again!' I therefore felt the best answer to Peter's statement was that cautious 'Ah' as obviously more was to come. And I was right. 'Guess what,' Peter went on. 'Harold Fielding had just offered me a blank cheque to appear in pantomime this Christmas at the Coliseum for six weeks.' The only reaction I could give to the news that Peter could name his own price was another single word. 'Oh.'

Peter gave a grin. 'And do you know what I just said to Harold Bloody Fielding?'

This time my vocabulary got bigger. 'No. What?' I said.

'Well,' said Pete, 'I said to Harold Bloody Fielding, I said, I told you to bugger off all those years ago, and I'm telling you to bugger off again now.'

Yes, status, position, power, even an unlimited salary—Peter just didn't care. It never bothered him and, in a way, this was his strength. People were aware of his indifference and, human nature being what it is, it threw them off balance. They were the ones who tried to convince Peter, he never had to convince them. No sitting on the edge of a chair hoping for the part. They sat on the edge of theirs begging him to work for them. I know for certain it wasn't a question of conceit. He really believed in destiny which, unfortunately, made him a sucker for every soothsayer and fortune teller on the face of the earth.

One of life's small, but worthwhile, pleasures is to see somebody who you know is either a fool or a charlatan fall, preferably publicly, flat on his or her face. This happened one wonderful night during a live television show from the London Palladium. Seated in the audience, and introduced from the stage, Maurice Woodruff, fortune teller and self-styled seer to the stars, was asked for a prediction. Eagerly leaping to his feet, the spotlight highlighting his simpering gloat, he firmly and deliberately assured several million TV viewers that the Labour party would undoubtedly lose the imminent general election. A few days later they won a resounding victory.

Unaffected by this public mortification he still went on collecting money from gullible people desperate to know their future. Gullible people who, unfortunately, included Peter. To me it was sad and pathetic that someone of Peter's calibre could fall under the influence of such a man. Pete was well aware of how I felt but his belief was, sadly, too deep, and Woodruff clung like a leech. The sinister side soon became apparent. As Pete's star rose, producers fawned on Woodruff and soon Peter was deciding to do such and such a film as Woodruff had definitely advised it.

* * *

My wedding took place on Sunday, 2 August 1959, at Marylebone Register Office at which, naturally, Peter and Anne were present. Typical of his love of gadgets, Peter brought an imposing array of glittering chrome which was a Hasselblad camera. Although known as the best camera in the world, it was obvious my friend had yet again not read the instruction books—the pictures he took were bloody awful. Fortunately, one of my brothers brought his modest 35mm camera, clicked away, and there is the record of a happy group of actors, all very youthful looking, all pulling the obligatory funny faces. Denis Selinger, the agent who represented both Peter and myself, had travelled all night from Scotland, to be my best man. That overnight journey gives some indication of a very generous gentleman who luckily, to this day, still looks after my professional life, and a lot of my private one too.

The carrying of the bride over the threshold

always looks so easy in romantic movies. Broad-shouldered leading men nonchalantly pick up their little brides and swing them through doorways with apparently no effort. I was determined to have a threshold to carry my bride over, so, the day before our wedding, I took possession of my first house. Luckily I found something that wasn't a confidence trick of a house agent. In their jargon the Des dtch res, three bd, own grg, spac gdn, immac con property was absolutely true, especially the immac con part.

Suffering the well-known pre-wedding desire to find a quick route to the Channel ports, I checked the house the day before the wedding. The nudge, nudge, I see you've got a king-sized bed, had been delivered. The television was working, and the gas, electric and water seemed to be fine. I'd bought the fitted carpets with the house and at least it had a furnished look. At three o'clock in the afternoon I opened the front door to see the biggest bouquet of flowers I'd ever seen had rung the bell. Lurking behind the flowers were Anne and Peter. 'Audrey's got to have a few flowers in the new house,' said Anne. They'd obviously bought out the entire stock of some local florists and while she filled the sink, and every other available vessel with water to put them in, Pete had a quick look round. We got a lot of his non-committal *Hmmns*. I learnt by years of experience that if they were quite well spaced out, accompanied by a lowered chin, it was good news. God help you if the tempo increased, and the chin was raised. Apart from finding a strand of cotton on the carpet in an upstairs bedroom, which he immediately picked up, the house had passed the test. I always seemed to bring out a strange parental attitude in Peter and him checking out the house to see all was well was quite par for the course.

Pete then made his standard excuse. 'Got to see someone,' he said and was gone. Anne had a look about, made her version of appreciative noises, then Peter was back. This time a huge cardboard box had rung the doorbell. We went through the ritual of 'Oh, you shouldn't have' and, as this was not the time for getting out the Stanley knife, I let Peter tear the box open. Finally, the best, up-market Hoover vacuum cleaner was revealed. At once we had to fix the 13 amp plug, check the fuse, and switch on. Half the carpet seemed to rise up off the underlay and Pete was satisfied. Desperate to find out what to get as a housewarming gift the strand of cotton had given him the clue. That cleaner became a strange bit of Peter's superstition. In years to come whenever he came to visit, whatever house we were living in, it was always 'How's the old vacuum, is it still working, and do you need a new one?' Shortly after Peter died I had it rebuilt, and it still works as well as the day it was bought. The mechanic who did the reconditioning work could have been a character invented by Peter himself. Flat cap, long alpaca coat, straggly moustache and steel-rimmed glasses. I'd told him it was a present and I wanted it restored. He gave it a pat. 'You're right to look after this, you know. Top of the range this was.' He gave it another pat. 'The feller what picked this knew what he was doin'.'

CHAPTER FIVE

THE PROPERTY HAS ARRIVED

A diary entry for Saturday, 16 April 1960, simply says 'New York'. It was, in fact, the start of a fairy-tale trip. It began, as things often did with Peter, with a simple phone call. Eventually I got used to these calls which always seemed to forewarn of important events, and there was a fascinating pattern to them. The more casual the call, the more significant the matter in hand. The theory seemed to be that if the approach was sufficiently nonchalant the less chance there was of rejection. In due course this nonchalance paid dividends as human nature usually dislikes the over-eager approach and Pete finally perfected the couldn't-care-less attitude. The call he made that mid-April was definitely of the tentative variety. 'Doing anything for the next couple of weeks?' he asked. I checked the diary. 'Well, I've got this Midday Music Hall broadcast on the 19th,' I said.

'Any chance of you getting out of it?' he replied.

Now, I never went in for the *Hmmns*. My reactions are more of a prolonged *Ssssss*, made by a sharp intake of the breath through the teeth. I made this noise, then said, 'Well, Pete, I am getting fifteen guineas!' I got a *Hmmn* in reply, then, after a pause he said, 'I would take it as a personal favour. You see, I've got to go to New York for a couple of weeks, all expenses paid, of course, and I've told them I won't go without you.' In those days we didn't have the high speed phone dialling we have now. You couldn't tap a number quickly on a keyboard. However, I think I set some sort of speed record with the old-fashioned dial getting through to the BBC and cancelling that broadcast.

Next, there was the question of visas. We were due to fly out on Saturday and this was Wednesday. After a few frantic phone calls we were told to report to the American Embassy in Grosvenor Square on Friday afternoon, the day before our flight. America, at that time, was still coming out of the horrendous Senator McCarthy era when Reds were imagined under the bed of every patriotic American and all immigrants were viewed with deep suspicion. Soberly clad in our dark suits we tried very hard to paint a picture of two true-blue Britishers, who would never think of tainting the shores of America with any kind of subversive propaganda.

Everything went fine until, after filling in all the necessary forms, we were ushered into a room which contained the largest desk I'd ever seen. It stretched halfway across the room, and behind it, sitting in solitary splendour, was a gentleman even more soberly dressed than us. He was wearing rimless glasses and at some time a scythe had apparently swept across the top of his head leaving his stiff, blond hair perfectly flat on top, making it look exactly like a shaving brush. A small propped-up board told us this was Vice-Consul Otis P. Coniff. On the wall behind his head, as a reminder of the power that he represented, was an enormous plaque of a giant eagle. Its beady eyes glared down, and its sharp, curved talons seemed prepared to rip you apart if you were stupid enough to get within striking distance.

Overawed by this demonstration of latent power, we sat silent while Otis P., with calculated importance, sorted through our papers, making an ostentatious rustling. He then brought the papers together and tapped them firmly downward on the desk. After checking that the bottom edge of every sheet of paper was exactly in line, Otis P. then gave a small double cough. This apparently was to warn us we were about to be inspected. He carefully looked at us in turn. 'Mr Stark?' I nodded. 'Mr Sellers?' Peter nodded. 'I would like you now both to raise your right hands and repeat after me.'

Dutifully we both obeyed and at first all went well. We both gave sincere, underplayed performances, and there was no doubt Otis P. was impressed. Impressed until we got to the bit about '... and I solemnly swear I do not intend to overthrow the American Government'. I concentrated like mad on one eye of the eagle, knowing that if I caught sight of Peter I'd be finished. Well, looking at the eye worked fine but it didn't make me deaf. On the word 'overthrow' Peter gave the tiniest choke and that was enough. I got the giggles, Peter had hysterics and Otis P. was not amused. In the end, we convinced him that it was only the thought of two English actors, merely intent on going to New York for a brief publicity campaign, taking on the might of America that had made us laugh and no disrespect was intended, but it was a bit touch and go.

The flight to New York was by Air France, on which the food came direct from Maxim's of Paris. High above the Atlantic, Pete and I, reclining in our first-class seats, watched as a glamorous stewardess flambéd crêpe suzettes; then, leaning close enough so her perfume had its full effect, said, in her divine, broken English, 'I 'ope you find this to your satisfaction.' New York was even better. The trip was the result of a full-page article in the *New York Times* announcing that a genius of an English actor, playing in no fewer than four films on Broadway, should be seen at all costs. This article was by the doyen of American critics, Bosley Crowther (with a status equivalent to our own Dilys Powell), who had noted that, quite by chance, Peter had four films currently playing in New York and had seen all four. His notice was ecstatic. The films included *I'm All Right, Jack*, in which Peter gave a marvellous performance as Kite, the trade union leader, spouting that immortal line 'all that ballet and waving corn', and *The Mouse That Roared*, where Peter, with a tin-pot army, took on the might of America.

All the pictures were big hits, and we smelt the sweet smell of success the moment the fleet of Cadillacs met us at the airport. Not one, not two, but three big, black limos glided into New York dropping us at the entrance to the Hamshere House hotel, right on Central Park. Peter and I climbed from one Cadillac while the other two disgorged a bevy of blue-suited, gleaming-toothed, showbiz executives and we all shot skyward to the penthouse suite.

Lucille Ball and Vivien Leigh were also currently staying at the hotel, but it was Peter who got the penthouse. As we walked in we saw even more blue-suited, gleaming-toothed executives, in serried ranks, all concentrating on making a good impression on that Oh-so-multi-talented-British Movie Star. I paused at the entrance and watched as they broke ranks and swarmed round Peter. Then another blue suit, lights glinting on the dentistry, picked up a white phone and uttered the line that became a catch-phrase for Peter and me for the rest of the time we were together. 'The property,' he said, 'has arrived.'

Property was the operative word. As far as those Americans were concerned here was a potential gold mine and whoever got to him first might grab himself a piece of the action. They crowded round what was to them a five-foot nine-inch dollar sign wearing horn-rimmed glasses and an amiable look on his face. Pete had every reason to look amiable. Even in our wildest dreams we never expected this treatment. They did everything but kneel and kiss his hand.

The next morning there was a knock on the door. Peter opened it and standing there, dressed in black bowler hat, white stiff collar and silver tie, dark sober suit and carrying a tightly furled black umbrella, stood the American actor Jules Munshin (always known to us as Julie). 'OK,' he said, in his best New York Brooklyn accent. 'Let's get down to Park Avenue and mingle wid them colonials.'

We fell on him with glee. Like a schoolboy he'd scoured New York for the right clothes to greet us. Julie, who epitomized everything that was best in American show business by being funny, generous, gloriously undisciplined and shrewd, all at the same time, had met Peter in England and it had been mutual attraction. And here he was, dressed for the occasion, ready to take us on our first tour of New York. And we really did stroll down the Avenue, the brass ferrule of Julie's brolly indicating all that really mattered in that socially conscious city. 'You can go in there,' he said, pointing to one restaurant. 'But unless you're lookin' for social suicide—' he pointed to another one—'make sure you stay outta there.' The morning was sunny, Park Avenue was filled with the fierce, assertive I'm-gonna-get-there-and-don't-you-try-to-stop-me New Yorkers, and that tall, bowler-hatted, wonderful, eccentric Julie Munshin stabbed at the air around him with his umbrella giving us the low-down. It was a great morning, and the trip had only just begun.

Now came the politics. Two separate film distributors, British Lion and the Walter Reade Company, were each handling two of the four current movies playing and were paying jointly for our trip. Both companies had PRs (public relations) whose job was to get maximum publicity out of Peter's visit and, with only twelve clear days' use of him, those PRs had to make sure not one important, precious moment was wasted. The problem that two companies were involved (after all, they were sharing the bill) was solved with a judgement worthy of Solomon. Each company would have us all to themselves on alternate days.

After mingling with the colonials we returned

to the Hamshere House where we were met by George. He was the PR for British Lion and they were obviously getting us for the first day. He was a large man, wearing a sandy beige suit with a slightly pinched waist. One limp hand gave a delighted downward arc as he saw Peter and, in a sibilant voice said, 'You do know—' a dramatic pause for effect—'*Everybody* wants to meet you!' The stress on the word everybody told us all about George. Apparently there was nobody in New York that George did not know. Nobody of any importance, that is. Even more to the point, there was nobody in New York that George did not have the full proverbial dirt on, and artfully he used this gossip as a commodity, trading it for other spicy bits of information. In the next twenty minutes we got a quick glossary of who was sleeping with whom, whose career was on the up, and who you didn't bother to talk to any more as they hadn't had a hit for the last few seasons. Finally George left, pausing dramatically at the door to make the startling declamation: 'Tonight, Sardi's!'

I looked at Peter, he looked at me, and at the same moment we both realized we were in for twelve days of sheer, unadulterated joy. And we weren't disappointed. The reverent tones George had used about Sardi's were well deserved. Even I'd heard of this mecca of New York showbiz. A restaurant that thrived on its glittering theatrical clientele and whose seating arrangements, organized by a head waiter who could spot a failure or success at thirty paces, was legendary. That night George unctuously led us into the famous room, walls festooned with photographs of every Broadway star, past and present, and we stopped at the obligatory rope that barred our further progress.

George looked at the figure guarding the rope. 'This,' he said with pride 'is . . .'. But he got no further. The guardian of the rope was not the head waiter of Sardi's for nothing. He cut George off short. '. . . Is *Mister* Peter Sellers!' he said. His stressing was even more masterly than George's. The verbal underlining of the word 'mister' was equivalent to conferring a knighthood on Peter. The rope was unhooked and Peter, myself, Julie and George were ushered to a corner that overlooked the room. 'Oh my God,' said George. 'You do realize we've got the *best* table in the room!'

So there it was. It took a head waiter in New York to make me realize this was a turning point. Up to then Pete was Pete. A carefree, comical lad. Now he was a valuable, must-be-carefully-nurtured asset that could make a lot of people a lot of money. As *Variety*, the bible of American showbiz, might have said, 'English Thesp Boffos Broadway'. Of course it could have just been the novelty, but I think Julie got it right. 'Pete, you bastard! I never got to this table before. Look at that,' he said. He pointed to a small table set back in a dark recess. 'You know who that is?' Well, of course we knew who it was. The face of the Tin Man from *The Wizard of Oz* peered anxiously round the room. 'Yeah, Ray Bolger. You know somethin'? He's a millionaire but they put him back there 'cos he ain't got what you got. He ain't got four pictures playing on Broadway. Come to think of it, he ain't got no picture playing anywhere.' I think Pete was expecting me to mention his gilded testicles but I fought back the temptation and let Julie have full flow. 'If you make it in Sardi's,' said Julie, 'you can make it anywhere.'

Out of the corner of my eye I could see the head waiter busy on the phone. He had that passing-of-information look on his face and, sure enough, during the course of our meal, no less than three of the top newspaper gossip columnists of New York joined our table. Told of Peter's presence they were there like lightning. The movie *The Sweet Smell of Success*, starring Burt Lancaster and Tony Curtis, summed up perfectly the power of these men. They strode across Sardi's knowing a mention from them could put you on a pinnacle. Ray Bolger and the rest of the clientele gave obsequious smirks but it was that British actor they'd come to see.

The next morning Miss Alrighty gave a

delighted squeal. 'Jesus Christ,' she said. 'Leonard Lyons gave you four inches!' This ambiguous remark simply meant that one of the major columnists had given Peter a lot of space. 'Last week,' she went on, 'he only gave Sinatra three.' These remarks came from a lady whose name Peter and I never remembered. We only knew her as Miss Alrighty as every other morning (she was the PR for Walter Reade) she came into the suite and said 'Alrighty?' before telling us the schedule of the day. Always before her appearance there would be an alarming rattle due to her habit of wearing masses of chunky jewellery. She also wore, day and night, a mink stole and a large flowered hat. She also had a heart of gold.

From the outset Miss Alrighty was completely baffled by the humour and behaviour of these two English actors. Try as she would she never really came to terms with what made Peter and me laugh. Every other day she frantically wanted to know what British Lion had arranged for us the day before. 'Oh my Gahd, you mean they took you to lunch at the Russian Tea Room, and then to the Four Seasons for dinner!' She got desperate as apparently all the venues for interviews started to dry up. Not able to recognize a leg-pull she stood, open-mouthed, as Pete and I poured salt on the wound. 'Oh yes,' said Pete. 'Beluga caviare followed by sturgeon ... and did we have wild strawberries, Gra?' I nodded. 'Smothered in fresh cream,' I said. 'And don't forget the oysters and the champagne at the Four Seasons!'

The low point of her association with us, however, came the night she took us to the apogee of the New York social scene, the 400 Club. It had all the trappings of the upper crust. Small tables, dim lights, discreet service and a head waiter who would have died rather than inform about the clientele to the riff-raff of newspaper columnists. Elegant small talk was the order of the evening until the coffee was ordered. 'Tea,' we said. 'May we have a cup of tea?' The merest frown passed over the head waiter's face, and two small cups of lukewarm water were placed before us, in each of which, looking like a large unhappy tadpole, lay a tea bag. The tea bag, with string attached, was bad enough. The fact that the string had a label telling us the tea was scented was too much. 'If only you'd kept some of those tea chests instead of throwing them into Boston Harbour we could have had some of that,' we said. Memories of hot, delicious cups of British tea came to our minds as Peter and I, to the mounting horror of Miss Alrighty, then set about showing the staff just how to make tea. Unflappably, a teapot was secured, God knows where from, and for the next fifteen minutes we held the restaurant in thrall as we demonstrated how the water had to boil, and how the pot had to be taken to the kettle and not the other way about. Any doubts Miss Alrighty had about our sanity were settled that night. We were beyond redemption.

But she and George were over the moon. There wasn't a newspaper, a radio show, or a TV station, that didn't want Peter. Jack Paar, the host of the biggest late-night TV show, had Peter as one of his guests and made sure millions of Americans knew New York was playing host to a brilliant new film comedian. He got everything but the ticket tape parade. Socially it wasn't bad either. Ken Tynan chain smoked and coughed his way through a long interview, but made amends by introducing us to Mike Nichols and Elaine May, who were the hottest comedy couple in New York.

Nichols, soon to be one of Hollywood's biggest directors, took a shine to Peter and we plotted an evening away from Miss Alrighty and George. Our hearts sank when Nichols told us we were going to Sardi's Uptown, but this was a different scene. There the non-striving-for-the-limelight actors hung out, and it was a great night. It was made for Peter when a dynamic lady bore down on our table and insisted Mike Nichols introduce her. This was Kay Thomson, one of the greatest cabaret performers in America. Peter, like most actors, found praise from a fellow performer the sweetest sound of all, and praise she certainly gave him. I always thought it was a pity that Peter never really took to the Americans because they certainly took to him.

As he was the head of one of the companies sponsoring our trip, it was obvious that we would spend one evening with Walter Reade. Now, I've found that very rich men, well aware of the power that money gives them, are inclined to talk slowly. This is probably something to do with people not wishing to interrupt them, particularly if they're picking up the bill. Walter Reade was very, very rich, very, very courteous and did, in fact, talk very, very slowly. 'Now, gentlemen . . .' he looked at both of us for some time. 'I know . . .' he transferred his gaze to Peter '. . . that you and . . .' the look swung to me '. . . Graham, must be . . .' he searched for the next word '. . . bored, meeting just actors, and . . .' he ventured a slight smile '. . . actresses.' The next sentence came in a comparative rush. 'Therefore I have arranged a party . . .' he raised a hand in anticipation of our effusive thanks '. . . for you both to meet some . . .' we both strained with him for the final words '. . . ordinary people.' With relief we sat back not knowing that Walter had just made one of the greatest understatements of the year.

We drove that night, passengers in his huge limo, and drew up outside a mansion on Long

Island that was just a little smaller than Citizen Kane's Xanadu. The driveway was filled with what looked like the entire output of the Cadillac factory for 1960, and large groups of uniformed chauffeurs stood and watched while Peter and I were taken in to meet the so-called ordinary people.

The two richest professions in New York are doctors and lawyers, and apparently every one of them was at Walter's party that night. They and their elegant wives. Nobody else. Possibly to Walter they were ordinary people but to Peter and me they hardly fitted that description. By the time we got there, the entire group were smashed out of their minds and Peter and I found ourselves in what would have made Peyton Place look like a kindergarten. Groping was rampant. In almost every alcove couples were locked in passionate embraces and it became obvious this was the start of the Long Island wife swapping season. Slightly smudged mascara eyelashes fluttered as several of the ladies, aware through their alcoholic haze that a couple of fresh male reinforcements had arrived, moved in to reconnoitre.

Peter and I had been parked, side by side, alone on a settee. We were not alone for long. The redhead that slid in, hip to hip, alongside me took a gulp at her glass then leant across and peered at Peter. 'We girls—' she loosely indicated the female group that had gathered around—'were told you were going to be here and I wanna tell we are all *so* mad about you British.' Peter gave a slightly embarrassed smile and a little squirm. The smile was because of the compliment, the squirm was because the blond who had wedged herself at his side was digging her nails into his thigh. It seemed as if the ordinary people were not about to waste any time. It was unfasten your seat belts, this is going to be a horizontal night.

Something divine in gold lamé, with a Cleopatra hairstyle, seated at Peter's feet, got rather intense. 'What did you do about those *bombs*?' she said.

'Ah yes, the bombs,' Peter replied and looked blank.

Cleopatra bit her lip. 'I mean, if they'd dropped them on me I'd have gone *right* out of my mind. Wouldn't you have done, Eunice?' The redhead at my side nodded 'Out of my mind,' she said, and emptied her glass.

'Ah, *those* bombs,' said Peter. He gave me a look and I knew we were away. If there was one thing in life Peter loved it was a situation like this and he grabbed at it. 'Well,' said Peter, 'one just had to deal with it, didn't one, Gra?' The line was perfect as, without effort, he had imperceptibly changed his voice, giving it an upper-class air of authority. In later years he was to use that self-same voice as the wing commander in *Dr Strangelove*—a performance which, in my opinion, even outshone the American President and the frenetic scientist he played in the same film. But here in Long Island that night it was the voice of a man who had faced danger in the skies above Britain, against the accursed Hun.

I followed Cleopatra's example and bit my lip knowing a lot of control in the near future would be needed. ''Course you know that Gra and I were both in the RAF,' Pete said. 'Sitting in those deckchairs on the drome all day. Just waiting for the scramble.' Obviously Peter felt our contribution to the Second World War, leaping about on makeshift stages while entertaining the troops on active service, was not as glamorous to those ladies as being a fighter pilot. Anyway, he always liked a bit of fantasy and I must say it was lovely stuff.

Now it was my turn. 'Saw Blackie the other day,' I said. 'Still got that dodgy leg. Bloody Me109. Came right out of the sun at him. Didn't stand a chance.'

Three pairs of scarlet lips parted in breathy delight as Peter and I refought the Battle of Britain. Heinkels and Dorniers dived in plumes of black smoke while pilots Sellers and Stark cleared the sky above old England. The fingernails dug even deeper into Peter's thigh, the crimson lips parted even further and Eunice's hand slipped under the back of my jacket, her fingers climbing slowly up my spine.

Well, we felt we had to bring a bit of glamour and excitement to the dreary lives of those very extraordinary ordinary people.

Back in New York Peter, with a fair bit of cunning, worked out that by trading in our very expensive first-class return air tickets Anne could fly out and join us for the last few days. Then the three of us could go back by sea on the *Queen Elizabeth*. 'Imagine,' he said. 'Five days of beef tea and shuffleboard.' A day later Anne flew in, and now Miss Alrighty and George had three English maniacs to deal with instead of two.

Our last night we celebrated by going to Trader Vic's, the famous Polynesian restaurant. Everything was fine until the list of drinks was handed to us. Anne gave a shriek of laughter and pointed. The printing was quite clear. Dr Funk Of Tahiti was the name of one of the drinks, and naturally that was the one we ordered. A large wooden bowl filled with a milky liquid was put in the middle of the table. From this harmless looking concoction three straws stuck out, one for each of us and, throughout the meal, we kept taking long sucks. It was sheer unadulterated bliss. At least it was bliss, but not so unadulterated. Lurking in that milky liquid was a strong lacing of rum, which has a delayed action. We decided to walk back to the hotel and as the New York air hit us, so did the rum. By the time we'd got back to our suite we were definitely tipsy and three grown people then sat up half the night, crying with laughter about the fictitious Dr Funk. No one can ever explain what makes you laugh but the image of a South Sea Island version of Major Bludnuk made our sides ache and tears run down our faces.

The next day the steward welcoming us aboard the *Queen Elizabeth* assured us that the sea voyage would soon put a little colour back into our obviously ashen cheeks. And it did. We had the shuffleboard, we drank the beef tea, we sat in our wooden chairs, legs well wrapped in tartan rugs, and loved every minute of it. Deciding to sail back on the *Queen E* was a masterstroke of Peter's as the massive ship was a total throwback to the 1930s. Time seemed to have stayed still since its launch. The décor, the string orchestra, the service, the food. Oh my God, the food. At breakfast you could eat any cereal manufactured, any bread you could think of, and your toast could be covered by at least 57 different varieties of marmalade. The menu seemed endless. The second day after sailing Peter and I got back to our cabins to find our dinner jackets laid out, sponged and pressed. Cufflinks and studs placed in our dress shirts. The gentlemanly way to remind you that, from the second night, evening dress was obligatory. A very civilized life.

In the game of one-upmanship Peter was a

formidable opponent, but came the morning on deck I did manage to upstage him. The Chief Purser himself came up and gave a salute. Not to Peter, not to Anne, but to me. 'Wireless Officer's compliments, Mr Stark. It seems there is a person-to-person telephone call for you from London. A certain Mr Peter Evans from the *Daily Express* wishes to converse with you.' Even a simple message like that was in 1930s language. Peter and Anne gave a whoop, sending me up rotten, but with just the touch of a swagger, I made my way to the wireless cabin. A transatlantic call in those days was really somcthing, but to get one at sea! It practically guaranteed you got invited to sit at the Captain's table. Peter Evans sounded as if he was shouting from Land's End through a megaphone. 'Did you take your camera, Graham?' he said.

'Never move without it,' I said.

'Right,' he said. 'We buy every roll of film you've taken. My boy will be at Southampton.'

My boy turned out to be a black-helmeted despatch rider who whisked the film up to London, and the next day a whole half-page of the *Daily Express* featured four pictures, taken by me, of Peter in various poses around New York. In one shot he was apparently conferring a knighthood on a waiter in our suite using a carving knife as the sword. Then, wearing skis, goggles and full winter sports clothes he was at the head of a flight of steps about to ski down into Grand Central Station. My favourite picture of all, which the *Express* featured the most was Pete, standing on the roof of a skyscraper wearing a huge white stetson, a giant cigar stuck in his mouth, a Polaroid camera slung round his neck, surveying the New York skyline with an arrogant look on his face as if saying, 'I'm gonna make this city mine!' which of course he had done. Those pictures set the seal on his triumph in New York and finally made the English film world realize that, in Peter, they really did have an international star.

Audrey was there to meet us, looking lovely, but with a rather anxious look on her face. I went to hug her and she pulled back. 'I don't think you better had,' she said. Anne tactfully looked the other way. 'Has something come between us?' I asked. She gave a nod and from under her coat brought a small tortoise. 'I bought you this,' she said. 'Coming home present.'

Peter took one look, gave its neck a stroke and said, 'I now pronounce you Dr Funk Of Tahiti.' Thirty years later Dr Funk is still waddling about our garden, always reminding us of that trip to New York.

CHAPTER SIX

'OW YOU LIKE A PUNCH UP THE FROAT?

To travel with Peter was to go strictly non-Baedeker. The only postilions that might be struck by lightning would be either customs officers who refused to wave him through, or travel agents who obstructed the smoothness of his voyage. Where they were concerned his fuse was very short. He did however sometimes provide additional services that you wouldn't get with Thomas Cook.

Along with a few million other people Peter adored Paris, particularly if he could stay at the Hotel Raphael. It was just up his street. Opulent, yet discreet, it reeked of French Empire. With its velvet drapes, and ornate gilt plasterwork, it had that upper-class naughtiness which only French hotels seem to have perfected. A short while after the return from New York Peter suggested we (he, Anne, Audrey and myself) have a weekend there. As Audrey and I never got the chance for a honeymoon I thought the idea was splendid, so off we went.

The flight was short, the chauffeur car at the airport to take us into Paris had the usual Gallic elegance, and the two adjoining suites at the Raphael were splendid. The connecting door between our suites was permanently open and, as we unpacked, Peter and I carried on a conversation in fractured French as to what we would do with our weekend. Maybe that night set in motion the extraordinary voice of Inspector Clouseau. 'Moi wishes to mange,' called out Pete. 'Très bon,' I replied. 'Avez-vous any idea about le situation of this mange?'

'Mais certainment,' he called again. 'Moi knows un beaucoup eating establishment where we can avez un diner grand!' And diner grand it was too. Phoning from his suite Peter got through to one of the best restaurants in Paris, booked a table and, while still on the telephone, arranged the whole menu as well.

Half an hour later yet another limousine glided off through the Paris traffic. Peter and I wore our dinner jackets while Audrey and Anne, both looking divine, had put on the full glamour, including their fur stoles: Anne's mink, and Audrey's arctic fox. The dinner was wonderful, the wine fantastic and, as if that wasn't enough, during the meal the roof of the restaurant was slid back to reveal a panorama of twinkling stars. There was nothing to top that. We had, however, forgotten that we were with Peter. As the coffee and liqueurs were finished he said, 'Right. Now for the Carrousel.' He looked at our three questioning faces and explained that this was the most famous transvestite club in Europe and had to be the place to visit.

Half an hour later we were sitting at a ringside table at the Carrousel and I was getting a bit worried as I found the third girl along in the chorus line rather attractive. I had every reason to be worried as the entire cast of the Carrousel show was male, dressed as ladies. And what ladies they were. Gorgeous creature after gorgeous creature danced and sang in front of us. 'I think I'll kill the blonde,' said Anne. 'Anyone with legs like that shouldn't be allowed loose.' While I was worrying about finding the third girl attractive Peter had other things on his mind. I noticed that the head waiter was lurking at his elbow. A plot was obviously afoot as bundles of franc notes were being pocketed by the waiter. Unobtrusively Pete gave us a sign and we quietly slipped out. Just by our car the doorman, resplendent in long uniform coat, with enormous epaulettes, joined the head waiter and Peter in more furtive whisperings. Anne gave a laugh. 'He'd better not be getting the phone number of anyone in that show!' she said.

As we climbed into the back seat the doorman, despite his epaulettes, managed to slide in the front seat beside the driver, muttered a direction, and away we went. For the second time that night Peter looked at three questioning faces. 'Well, you can't come to Paris without seeing an exhibition,' he said. The noise Anne made was a sort of strangled *Aaagh*, Audrey just opened her mouth, and I thought it best to put my expression into neutral. Down winding back streets we went until we pulled up in a sleazy street outside a sleazy bar, and the four of us climbed out onto a sleazy pavement.

Epaulettes took us into the estaminet which was straight out of Simenon. Thick Gauloise smoke, a few customers obviously just returned from Devil's Island, and a beaded curtain half parted by a small fat Madame. She coyly beckoned. Epaulettes gave a smirk, pocketed more francs and disappeared. We passed through the curtain as the Madame primped her ginger hair with small, plump, bejewelled hands, obviously convinced by our appearance that we were the English lords and ladies. She got straight to business. 'You laike pretty girl?' Pete nodded. ''Ow many pretty girl you laike?' Peter held up two fingers. Her plump hands clapped and three girls filed in. One redhead, one brunette, one blonde. 'Flags of all nations,' said Peter. Anne hit him.

The Madame now realized that Peter, by his casual manner, was obviously not an English lord. More likely an English Duke. She fawned. 'Your 'Ighness, weech two girls you laike?'

Pete looked at me. 'How about the blonde and the brunette, Gra?' My neutral face got even more neutral and I looked at my shoes. 'Right,' said Peter. 'Blonde and brunette it is.'

Dismissing the redhead with a wave of her hand the Madame gave a coy simper, 'Now, you weesh to parteecepate?'

Pete shook his head. 'Certainement not,' he said. 'We wish merely to regarde.'

The room at the back of the curtain was quite small but the bedroom was even smaller, and the large brass double bed that was in it didn't help. The Madame glared at the room as if it gave her personal affront. '*Merde*!' she said dramatically. ''Ow are they supposed to seet?' Four small gilt chairs appeared like magic and there was just enough room to place them in a row alongside the bed. Madame then begged us to sit, told the girls to be good, and vanished.

Making a quick-change artist look a bit slow off the mark both girls were naked in moments and dived on the bed. The four of us were now sitting in a cramped row, with our knees pressed tight to the bed while the two naked girls went into their standard routine. I tried hard to look at the ceiling and failed miserably. Anne and Audrey wore identical expressions of disbelief, while Peter, totally relaxed, was obviously enjoying every moment of it. Suddenly the small blonde girl, who up to then had been going through the motions in a rather bored manner, gave a start, raised one of the dark girl's legs that was obstructing her view, pointed at Peter and cried, '*Un grand acteur de cinéma anglais*!'

From that moment on it got hysterical. Both girls, thrilled they had such an esteemed film star as an audience, gave their all. To say they flung themselves into their work would be an understatement. We got girlish giggles, arch looks and, as a finale, a comedy routine demonstrating how various nationalities had sex. It was a *tour de force*. We had to give them applause and, if we hadn't been wedged so tight, Pete and I might have given them a standing ovation. Everybody shook hands and the two girls let forth a torrent of excitable French. The Madame was beside herself. Translating she said, 'The girls weesh me to tell you they 'ave never 'ad such an audience, and 'ope it is not too long before you wish to view them once more.'

* * *

Pete never did things by halves. Not long before the trip to America he'd decided the country gent was the life for him so he bought the Manor House at Chipperfield. It was the ultimate cliché English country residence. Oak beams and rustic brick, surrounded by acres of mature green lawns, and boasting a tree that

Queen Elizabeth I was reputed to have strolled under. I don't remember saying it but Michael, Peter's son, swears that the first time I set eyes on it I asked Pete why hadn't he bought Buckingham Palace while he was about it. But it was very beautiful.

The early summer, after our return from New York, was glorious, and at Chipperfield, every weekend, white-coated waiters were busy handing out drinks to favourite friends as we lounged by the swimming pool. Every so often John and Roy Boulting would arrive. Alternating as director and producer, the twin brothers had made some of the most successful films ever to come out of England, and had also been instrumental in giving Peter one of his greatest successes with *I'm All Right, Jack*. They were also cricket maniacs and would appear, laden with pads, stumps, bats and the whole paraphernalia of what they considered not just a game, but a religion.

They would always insist we stop the indolence round the pool and concentrate on the importance of being true-blue Britishers by buckling on the pads and putting willow to leather. Teams were drawn up, stumps pounded into the grass, and highly organized matches were played. Unfortunately a young American was one of the most regular guests, and being a natural sportsman, with the eye of an eagle, he used to demolish John and Roy's bowling. To rub salt in the wound he explained he'd been brought up on baseball. 'Gee,' he said. 'The ball is so much easier to hit now you've given me this broader bat.' The cricket ball soared skywards with monotonous regularity. Finally John and Roy called an emergency meeting of their side, which included Peter, Dave Lodge, John Le Mesurier and me. As we clustered conspiratorially in the long grass, John Boulting declared that the American must be got out at all costs. 'Remember, gentlemen,' he declaimed in his clear, upper-class voice. 'It's a question of honour. Even if we have to cheat.'

We'd have dinner in the dining room, which was a miniature baronial hall, and the huge living room was equipped with the very best hi-fi where Pete and I could sit and play our mutual love, jazz records. I marvelled at the sound but, unfortunately, Peter was always convinced that somewhere someone had made, or was in the process of making, a camera with a sharper lens than he had, a more superior car than he had, or a more sensitive piece of hi-fi equipment than he had. This did not bring him peace of mind. I'd sit there going mad about Count Basie, while Peter sat there going mad about the state of his woofers and tweeters.

This could have been the reason why the next time I heard jazz at Chipperfield was not via speakers but live, in the flesh. To celebrate the opening of his latest venture, the rebuilding of the large barn in the grounds, Peter laid on a party with the conventional food and drink plus music to dance to. But no sign of long playing records, or tape decks. Sitting in a group at the end of the barn were five of the very best jazz musicians in the country. Kenny Baker on trumpet, Duncan Lamont on tenor sax, Lenny Bush bass, Alan Clare piano and Tony Crombie on drums. A fantastic night of jazz followed and, as part of the night's festivities, Peter sat in as deputy to Tony Crombie and proved that, where drumming was concerned, he could hold his own with the best.

That particular year I was making a film at Pinewood Studios called *Launcelot and Guinivere*, directed by Cornel Wilde, in which I played a scruffy retainer at the court of King Arthur. One afternoon, walking down the long corridor that led from the film sets to the dressing rooms, wearing my wrinkled tights and dishevelled wig I saw, far in the distance, a portly figure advancing slowly towards me. The figure got nearer and, beneath a battered straw hat, was the amiable face of Leo McKern. He took in my broken-down appearance then indicated his own threadbare, tatty suit. 'Let's face it, dear boy, you and I will never get the scornful parts, only the grovelling ones.'

I never forgot that wonderful line of Leo's. Nature designs you, and casting directors follow. Mentally you might be equipped to play Hamlet, but physically you get stuck with the Gravedigger, which is probably why Wolf Mankowitz, who had scripted the film of *The Millionairess*, based on the famous Bernard Shaw play, booked me to appear as the butler. Definitely a grovelling part. Peter was delighted (he was starring in the film, as the shy, diffident Indian doctor) and a couple of weeks after I'd been cast we had a pre-picture party at Chipperfield.

'She's sitting over there,' said Pete knowing perfectly well there was one person I wanted to meet at that party more than anyone else. For days, the popular press had tantalized their readers with news that Sophia Loren was coming to England to play the title role in the film; I bathed in the reflected glory that I was going to appear with her. She sat very gracefully in a chair placed out on the lawn, wearing a ravishing hat and the smile that had driven most of the world's male population mad. Pete made one of his most charming introductions. 'Soph,' he said. 'This is Gra. He's playing your butler.' He then walked off and left us alone. To her eternal credit Sophia never blinked an eyelid. Obviously she presumed this was the way Englishmen introduced each other and, politely giving me another blinding smile, said, 'I 'ear you 'ave been to Amereeka. What you theenk of

Amereeka?'

I told her I loved it but had been put off by the waiters at the Four Seasons restaurant, who, dressed in full livery, insist on bowing low before handing you a menu almost too big for you to hold—then spoil it by saying 'Yeah?' She gave a scream of laughter, drummed her feet on the ground and said, 'Eet's so true!' I was her slave for life.

The first day on any film is always nerve-racking. Luckily you find you know quite a few of the crew and there's lot of 'Cor, how come they let you play this part?' Pete was there, wishing everyone luck. He wasn't shooting that day. I was. In fact I was in the first scene after the credit titles, and in the make-up chair that morning, the hairdresser sidled up behind me, looked at my scalp, and didn't do a lot for my confidence by suggesting to the make-up man that a bit of eyebrow pencil on the hair line might be quite a good idea. In his turn the make-up man moved in and peered closely at my nose. 'Any chance of you acting with your chin up a bit?' he said. 'I'm worried about that large shadow on your upper lip.'

The film opened with two minutes of credits, which rolled over a static shot of two huge black and gold doors. At the end of the two minutes the doors slid open and there I stood, as the butler, silver salver balanced on one hand. A pause, then I walked through the doors towards the camera. End of shot. Nice and easy, nothing to worry about. I had not counted on Sophia. All through the nerve-racking, seemingly endless, two minutes behind those doors Sophia kept looking at the silver salver and whispering to me, 'You know you're agoing to drop eet!' She was divine.

The director Anthony Asquith was also divine, especially when he kept putting on Sophia's hats and twirling round the set in them. '*This* is the way you should do it!' he would say, stamping his foot.

Pete and I decided Sophia should have the last word. We both gave her a crash course in cockney rhyming slang. 'Watch my lips,' Peter said. 'Ball of chalk is walk, so you go for a ball. Pig's ear is beer, so you have a pint of pigs.' She was a natural. In days we had her well trained, and on one memorable morning she faced Anthony Asquith, her hands on those beautiful hips, her face close to his. 'Ow you like,' she said, 'a bunch of fives right up the froat?' In other words, how would he like a punch on the chin? The crew gave a cheer, Asquith fell about laughing, while on the sidelines Peter and I gave nods of approval. Professor Higgins could have done no better.

Anthony Asquith was in fact a marvellous director and he was getting a brilliant comic performance from Peter as the gentle Indian doctor whom the millionairess falls in love with.

Sophia was heaven, occasionally popping her head out and saying 'Yeah!' to me during scenes, and all in all it was a very smooth, happy film. Until, that is Peter told me that he and Sophia were in love.

I was walking onto the stage one day when suddenly he appeared, as if out of nowhere, grabbed my arm, and pulled me behind a piece of scenery where, obviously, he had been hiding. 'I've been waiting for you, Gra. Got to talk to you.' His voice was very low, almost a whisper. 'It's me and Sophia. I'm in love with her, and she's in love with me.' He put his hand on his chest in a pathetic way, his face crinkled, and he seemed to be about to cry. 'Imagine, Sophia Loren in love with me.' Now, when your best friend tells you that one of the most beautiful women in the world is in love with him you're not supposed to feel sorry for him. But I'm afraid I did. I also remember thinking to myself, 'Oh Christ, now what do we do?'

The film continued, as films do. Sophia was a professional to her finger tips. In one scene I stood, as her butler, waiting to wrap her in a rug, as she climbed, soaking wet, out of the river into which she had previously jumped. To get the maximum drowned-rat effect the director got Sophia to lie for several minutes, fully dressed, in a bath of cold water. Mechanical failures meant that we had to do the scene five times. She never complained. Five times she went back into her caravan, changed her clothes, and five times lay back in that bath of cold water. No director could ask for more.

As the film progressed, Peter kept finding excuses for us to talk. Well, he did all the talking really. Each day I got details of how the affair was progressing, and each day he kept shaking his head in disbelief. 'It can't be true. It just can't be true.' The fantasy world that Peter so often lived in had apparently come true to life. This beautiful woman, desired and adored by millions, had fallen for him. I was given details of furtive meetings, of passion in the dressing room and even awkward (I would have thought totally impossible) gymnastics in the back seats of parked cars. I got it all. It was, to say the least, embarrassing. Peter felt he had to tell somebody; I just wished it didn't have to be me. Strangely enough, though, throughout it all, there was a nagging doubt, a suspicion that things were not quite what they seemed. But he told me he was glad he had a friend to tell his secret to.

The dictionary definition of secret is information shared confidentially. Obviously Peter had not looked at his *Concise Oxford* recently as the next thing I knew was that he'd faced Anne, at Chipperfield, and revealed all.

The effect was predictable. Anne, with the time-honoured reaction of a wife displaced in her husband's affections, moved out. The suitcases were packed, she drove her car to our door, and in our spare room she unpacked.

From our first meeting, Anne and I had found it easy to talk. We also shared a sense of humour and her delicious laugh was infectious. As she and Audrey also got on so well it made life easy socially. The memorable trip to Paris, during which the four of us had such a wonderful time, had bound us together. It was a nasty shock when Anne came and asked to stay as it implied a possible permanent separation, but there was a chance we might be able to get them back together again. The first night Anne was at the house, Audrey, knowing how close I was to Peter, and how long I had known Anne, tactfully left us alone, which gave Anne a chance to unburden herself.

Sitting in an armchair in the lounge she looked as pretty as ever, but was clearly under great strain. Little by little she began to talk. I mainly remember how dignified she was. If I expected tears I never got them. Then she uttered a line that could have come straight from Dorothy Parker. 'You know what,' she said, referring to Peter's confession. 'The bastard only told me because he couldn't be bothered to have a bad conscience.' And because I laughed, she laughed too. I think that was when I realized there might be a chance.

We then had a week of Peter coming nightly to the house and formally asking our permission to take Anne out if, of course, she agreed. Like a Victorian father I put Peter in the lounge while Audrey checked upstairs with Anne. We did everything but say 'And we want her back by midnight.' Gradually the separation began to do the trick. Peter was on his very best behaviour and Anne, after about a week, moved back to Chipperfield and things went back to relative normality. But it had been a close shave.

★ ★ ★

Pete had already made a hit record 'Ying Tong Iddle I Po', which was a huge best-seller. That September of 1960 George Martin, who went on to achieve fame as the producer of the Beatles' records, decided to make a double-sided 45 rpm, starring Peter. Side A was an interview, by me, of Peter playing the founder of the Flat Earth Society. It was a funny script by Munro-Smith and Pete came up with one of his tortured eccentric voices. He told me it was based on his gardener who had the wonderfully rustic name of Dewberry. The Flat Earth founder, with his earthy, gasping voice had a wonderful dimension as he raved on about his horror of all things round. Balls, bottoms, breasts, the names poured out, and the interview was hilarious. So good in fact that George said, 'We've got to do something else for the other side of the record.'

By this time Pete had invented a fictitious German Swing Band Leader, Kurt Augerschlagen from Radio Spundfunk. He was a glorious send-up of those hearty, American-obsessed, band leaders who, always dressed in a white suit, with a baton two foot long, stood in front of huge glittering swing bands oozing charm, and playing terrible music. 'Right, Gra,' Peter said. 'Let's do another interview. Kurt on BBC Jazz Night.' We roughly plotted it, the sound man started the tape, and off we went. The voice he used was marvellous. Subtly it incorporated a strong American slant, trotting out the jazz clichés like, 'I haff to say it's really groofy,' and 'Man, being here mit you is a real gas.' Up in the control box George Martin was grinning from ear to ear as on we went. My character, loosely based on famed radio jazz expert, Steve Race, started probing into Kurt Augerschlagen's past. As he'd played in the forces during the war, listeners would like to know how the orchestra had time to rehearse. A special unit? What would that be? Gradually, boxed into a corner, Kurt exploded and, with the same intensity that he would use two years later as Dr Strangelove, Peter went into his final speech. 'You bloody British. So vat iff we had this leedle special camp. We vas only doing vat all the ze camps were doing, but on a smaller scale. Anyvay, you try playing a saxophone mit all that smoke!' Needless to say, that B side recording never left the studio.

Also in that year Peter took the plunge and directed his first movie, *Mr Topaze*. He planned for me to be in the film with him, but by that time I was doing the Art Buchwald revue, *The Art of Living*, at the Criterion in London, and also filming during the day, so it just wasn't possible. But Audrey and I had plenty of time to see Peter and Anne at Chipperfield, and gradually we slipped back into the routine that had existed before *The Millionairess*.

CHAPTER SEVEN

I AM OBLIGED TO SAY I AM RECEIVING MUCH PLEASURE

If ever the grovelling-part label suited anything it suited the role I next played alongside Peter in the film *Only Two Can Play*. He played a frustrated Welsh librarian; I played a dirty little man haunting the public library, peering through every book looking for the naughty bits. It was a character-actor's dream part. My clothing could have played it without me, as the raincoat they gave me stood up on its own. With glee I told Peter I was even going to work in the twitch that he wasn't allowed to have in our first film together. Dishevelled, unshaven, disreputable, I hid round a corner one wet Sunday in Swansea, twitching away and waiting for the word 'Action' from the director. I had to be round the corner so I could make an entrance. The policeman didn't believe a word of it. He was very large, very Welsh, and proud of his beautiful Swansea. 'If you're not out of 'ere in two minutes I'll 'ave you,' he said. 'We got film people down yere, from London, an I don't want nasty little buggers like you 'angin about.'

Peter's part didn't need any make-up as,

visually, he was almost playing himself, with a Welsh accent of course. We did most of the shooting at Twickenham Studios and, as usual, we sat every lunchtime going through the hell of watching what are known as the 'rushes', the film you shot the day before. To watch rushes with a film crew is a joy to behold. A tiny patch of perspiration on a forehead and you hear the make-up girl give a moan; the smallest shadow on a door the lighting cameraman has a heart attack, and if there's a judder on a zoom, the camera operator decides to emigrate. Each of the crew gazes intently at the area they are concerned with and suffers tortures at what they see wrong. The worst sufferers are the actors. There, in sharp focus, on a large screen, is every movement, look, and gesture magnified a dozen times. What yesterday you thought was elegant underplaying, today is revealed as manic, grotesque face pulling. Like the crew concentrating solely on their work, you concentrate solely on yourself. Not a happy experience.

One particular day the rushes featured Ken Griffiths, a brilliant Welsh actor, giving a very funny performance as a comic Uriah Heep. He had a late call so he wasn't at the screening. However, as we blinked our way into the daylight, he came in the studio gates. At once Peter pounced. 'Right,' he said. 'Just how much did you pay? Go on, tell me.'

Kenny's jaw dropped. 'Pay what,' he said in his own splendidly sibilant Welsh accent.

'Close-up money, that's what,' said Peter. 'You can't see anybody but you up on the screen.' He leant closer. 'You've been bribing the cameraman, Kenny boy, that's what you've been doing.'

Kenny's face was a picture. 'Oooh, I wouldn't do that, Pete boyo. You know I wouldn't.'

But Pete didn't give up. 'What's more,' he said, 'I think there's been a bit of a back-hander to the sound department as well. You're the only one you can hear properly.'

Kenneth looked as if he was going to have a seizure. Now it was nose to nose with Peter. 'How dare you suggest I would stoop so low as to give a back-'ander.' Then there was the briefest moment, a magic pause, before he spoke again. 'Purely as a matter of interest,' he said, 'what's the going rate?'

Yes, we had a lot of laughs but there was always another side to Peter. It often seemed that he had to take a dislike to someone and, for no reason that anyone could ever understand, it happened on this occasion to be Virginia Maskell. Gentle and kind, every inch a lady, this lovely actress was playing his wife in *Only Two Can Play* and he tried every ploy to get her out of the picture. Fortunately the Boulting Brothers, who were producing the film, prevailed, and to this day you can see her giving a very moving performance. Even more bizarre was that, having completed the film, Peter took such a dislike to it that he sold out his share of the profits. It went on to break every box-office record in the country. I loved him dearly but in business, I'm afraid, he just didn't have a clue.

Just before making *Only Two Can Play* Peter had worked on *Lolita* with a director who was to have an enormous influence on him. Young Stanley Kubrick had originally been an *enfant terrible* in the American cinema but now, as Stanley Kubrick, director, with *The Killing* and *Paths of Glory* to his credit, he started, with his producer and partner, Jimmy Harris, to make some of the most notable films ever to come out of Europe. The performance he got out of Peter in *Lolita* was nothing short of magical. He sensed at once Peter's ability to ad lib dialogue, and create visual comedy, and he capitalized on it. As Clare Quilty, villainy personified, Peter gave one of the black comedy performances of the year, and it seemed as if there was no limit to the range of characters he could play.

Over several dinners at Chipperfield, Audrey and I met Stanley and his wife, German actress Christiana Kaufman. Audrey, Christiana, Stanley and I became close friends, and their presence, as well as that of other people from the film, soon brought back a sense of fun to the house and the dinners became occasions to look forward to. Gradually the areas became defined. Peter, at his end of the table, deep in conversation with Stanley about films, Christiana occupying the middle ground with Audrey, debating art, flowers and children (she later became godmother to our youngest son), while up at the other end of the table would be Anne, myself, and any one of the guests who Anne felt could make her laugh. She was trying very hard to blot out *The Millionairess* episode and seemed to be succeeding.

One of the regulars at the laughter end of the table suddenly turned up at my house one afternoon. We knew each other pretty well so the visit wasn't surprising. What was surprising was the slim, elegant, executive suitcase he placed on the table. Then, in a quiet voice, he spoke one of those terse, yet meaningful lines beloved of writers of B movies. 'She's picking that up on Tuesday,' he said.

'It would help a great deal,' I replied, 'if I knew who "she" was.'

He shook his head. 'Sorry, I somehow thought you might have guessed. Anne, would you give that to Anne.'

I looked out of the window—always a good 'gain time' ploy—then looked back at him. 'You can't pass it over yourself then?'

He shook his head again. 'I'm flying to LA tomorrow.'

Now it is a fact that the moment we start

getting serious we start talking pedantically. Perhaps instinct tells us we should, at such times, make ourselves absolutely clear. 'If,' I said, 'I am being asked to pass on said case to my best friend's wife, I think I should, first of all, be told what is in it.'

The friend was briefer than me. 'Five thousand pounds,' he said.

I did the looking out of the window bit again and, high in the sky, saw four long vapour trails streaming from the rear of a tiny silver jet. The penny finally dropped.

I then explained, as gently as I could, that I didn't really feel aiding my best friend's wife to leave the country was quite the thing to do. 'I mean, we were in the Air Force together.' Lost for words I found myself pointing at two huge hi-fi speakers. 'He gave me those only a few weeks ago. What I'm trying to say is . . .'

To his eternal credit the friend gave a grin, albeit a wry one, and picked up the case. 'I shouldn't have asked. See you soon,' and, with an exit that must have taken some effort to make, left the house.

Well before next Tuesday I telephoned Anne and she came round. I told her what had happened. She sat for a while without speaking then suddenly said, 'You're absolutely right. I shan't be going to Los Angeles.' Then she added, 'I think I'll always be grateful.' She gave one of her grins. 'You know nothing happened, don't you?' I nodded because I knew that too.

Anne went back to Chipperfield and told Peter all that had happened. Peter of course had heard the laughter, watched the fun at the other end of the table, and for a while he even imagined I was playing some sort of go-between role. A day later he came by. He sat in the same chair Anne had sat in and we had a lot of *Hmmns*. Finally he managed to get it out. 'Thanks a lot, Gra,' he said.

A short while later Peter made one of his laconic phone calls. 'Come to dinner tonight. You and Aug. Got something to tell you.' During the meal at Chipperfield he gave a rather self-satisfied smile. 'Ever see a play called *Dock Brief*?' he asked. 'John Mortimer. Sensational. Only two parts. Going to be a film. I play one part . . .' He was enough of an actor to give himself pause for the final effect. '. . . and you're playing the other.' He gave a triumphant smile. Anne gave a nice smile too. I knew what it was all about, of course. This was the reward. I'd done the decent thing by my friend and now he was doing the decent thing by me, but I knew it wasn't going to happen. With only two people in the film it was obvious the distributors would demand, and rightly so, another star name above the title, and they got it. Two weeks later Peter broke the news that Richard Attenborough would be playing the part. Which he did and, I regret to say, gave an absolutely wonderful performance.

* * *

Twice that summer I sang on television. For someone who is not only tone deaf but has been known to change key several times in one chorus, it must be some sort of record. Mind you, the people I sang with helped. The first duet was with Patti Page as, back with the grovelling parts, I played her butler in a TV special. Miss Page had sold several million records and after listening to her that night I wasn't surprised. Fortunately she had a nice loud voice that drowned me out. The very next week I went into rehearsal with Peter and someone who had sold even more records than Patti Page. This was Jo Stafford. I had a duet with her as well and again luck was on my side and she had an even louder voice. But the high spot of the TV show was playing a sketch with Peter that remained one of our favourites. The recruiting sergeant from World War One (Peter) terrifying a young civilian (me) into joining up. Peter, ferociously twirling a pace stick, and wearing a walrus moustache, managed to be more frightening than the famous Kitchener poster we had in the background.

I went briefly to Italy to make a film, *Village of Daughters*. On my return, paying a visit to

Chipperfield, I found the rooms filled with removal men stuffing newspaper-wrapped vases into tea chests. The furniture was swathed in dust sheets. Sadly the lovely days at Chipperfield were no more. Peter was on the move. Determined to start afresh he'd bought a grandiose apartment, high in a prestige block of flats overlooking Hampstead Heath and, had he known it, he couldn't have done anything worse. While the apartment was being prepared he and Anne, with the children, moved into a suite at a luxury hotel in Knightsbridge, the Carlton Tower.

It was modern and sumptuous but still a hotel suite. Christmas time the floor was strewn with mounds of unopened presents for the children as half the producers in London sent gifts to Michael and Sarah, hoping to influence Peter. Unopened boxes were trampled on, or even thrown away. No child could get through them.

In January 1962 we had the première of *Only Two Can Play*, and the film was a huge success. The run of hit films for Peter seemed unending. In the foyer of the London Pavilion I got a hug from Virginia Maskell. Sadly I never saw her again as some time later she tragically took her own life.

By now the new flat in Hampstead was ready. Every wall was clad in never-ending dark rosewood and I found the whole effect very depressing. But I quite liked the interior designer who'd been responsible, Ted Levy, an amiable South African architect. As usual Peter had filled every room with gadgets, and his latest toy was the tape recorder to end all tape recorders. It was on this that he and I made a recording one afternoon for a new LP. We both sat back in armchairs, each with a stereo mike, did it in one take, and decided this was the only way to work.

Next day Major Bludnuk was on the line. 'My dear Starky, it seems you have left a box, in the plain brown wrapper of course, at my humble abode. Perhaps you would care to retrieve it!' I didn't know what he was talking about so I went round. Majestically occupying the centre of the dining room table was the largest most opulent camera case I'd ever seen. The huge hammered metal box effortlessly opened and there, nestling in fitted red velvet, was one of the most beautiful camera outfits in the world. A Linhof Mark IV, with a set of matched lenses and all accessories. It was like winning the camera pools. Peter, a grin on his face watched my reaction. 'Gawd Almighty,' I said.

'Actually it's Pelling and Cross,' he replied. 'Saw it in their window, realized you'd done me a favour with the recording, thought you'd like it.' Feeling unable to discuss a fee with me for doing the recording Pete had done the next best thing and was paying me in kind. The camera outfit was worth at least five times what I would have expected to be paid for such a job.

Unfortunately the move to Hampstead didn't solve Peter and Anne's problems. She had loved Chipperfield and, had they stayed there, I think things might have been all right, but soon Peter and Anne finally parted. The gossip columnists had a field day, particularly when Anne's name became linked with that of Ted Levy, the architect of the new flat but, as he and Anne genuinely fell in love, got married, had a child, and lived very happily until Ted's sad death in 1986, this nastincss soon got knocked on the head.

Peter went potty, but in fairness no more than many other parties in a marriage that has gone sour. A line from the film that won Bing Crosby his Oscar always stuck in my mind. 'In divorce,' Crosby's character said, 'the loser always goes for the groin.' And Peter was the loser, and well he knew it.

One thing that did console him at this time was the appearance on the scene of the Great Bert. This was what soon became our nickname for Bert Mortimer, and never was a title more fitting. Originally just engaged as Peter's driver, he rapidly proved himself a modern version of the Admirable Crichton. As well as being an aide-de-camp, and general dogsbody, he was also Peter's loyal and faithful friend for the next sixteen years. Bert had been Cary Grant's driver for a long while but as Grant was now returning, more or less permanently, to America, Bert was available and, sensibly Peter snapped him up.

I first began to appreciate his value on the day Pete, Bert and I collected a golden labrador puppy, which Audrey and I had given Pete's children Michael and Sarah, from the vet's in Chelsea. It had just had an injection. Bert carefully placed the little dog on the back seat of Pete's Rolls-Royce, where the children were already sitting, and got into the driving seat with Pete beside him. I had my own car so slowly we drove away in procession, me at the rear. Two hundred feet down the road the Rolls's brake lights flared on and the car jerked to a stop. All four doors flew open simultaneously and in perfect unison all four occupants of the car, with looks of horror on their faces, leapt out. It was a comedy routine worthy of one of the *Panthers*. I braked, Pete ran back to my car. 'Shit,' he declaimed. 'Dog shit. All over the back seat of the car!'

Pete rang the doorbell of a nearby house and a rather well-dressed, aristocratic man opened the door and, in a very upper-class voice, said, 'May I help you?'

Without a pause Peter became an officer of the Guards. 'Just wonderin', any chance of a bucket of warm water and a scrubbin' brush, what?'

The man took a pair of spectacles from his breast pocket, put them on, and peered at Peter's feet. 'Oh I say, stepped in a bit of the ... er ... you know?'

Pete's polite laugh was straight out of *Burke's Peerage*. 'Oh gosh no,' he said. 'The ... er ... you know is on the back seat of my Rolls.'

Bert did the cleaning up, and greater love hath no man for his employer than he cleaneth up dog mess from the back of his Rolls-Royce.

* * *

Nostalgia in Peter became stronger by the day, particularly now he was on his own. He made a person-to-person call from Paris begging Audrey and me to have a weekend there with him while he was filming *The Waltz of the Toreadors*. 'I'm at the Raphael,' he said. 'And I can get you the same suite you had last time, right next to me.' We couldn't really say no.

Like an excited boy he met us in the lobby, took us upstairs, and it was just the same as the last time. Even to the shouted conversation through the connecting doors. 'Moi has une jolie femme fatale joining us for le diner,' Pete called out. 'In fact moi must say she is a très jolie femme fatale.' His description fitted Dany Robin to perfection. This exquisite French actress was playing opposite Peter in the film.

Petite and delightful, she made us laugh all through the meal with her broken English. Every time she had a sip of wine she made a remark which Peter and I never tired of quoting to each other: 'I'm obliged to say that I am receiving much pleasure from this.'

She invited the three of us to spend the next day at her house outside Paris where she lived with her husband who was himself a well-known French film actor. They were mad about animals and had a baby crocodile that lay on a rock, in the middle of a small pool, wearing a permanent grin. But her pride and joy was the huge pelican called Alfred who was free to wander about the house at will. His wingspan filled the corridor and if you didn't get out of his way he was quite liable to give you a whack with his huge bill.

As Audrey and I were flying back the next morning, Dany agreed to join us again for dinner that night. At the Raphael Peter and I waited in the bar for Audrey to come down from the suite, and Dany to arrive in her car. In that brief time Peter repeated, almost word for word, what he had told me about Sophia, only this time he was talking about Dany. 'You see,' Pete said, 'I'm in love with her, and she's in love with me.' Then came the physical bits. Admittedly we didn't get the back of the car, but he did describe a lot of action in the dressing room.

The dinner was a great success. Dany was as funny and delightful as ever. At the end of the evening, back at the Raphael, we had coffee up in the suites and half-way through Pete got a business call from London, and went into the other room. At once Dany was out of her chair and, moving close to Audrey and me, whispered frantically, 'Please, I beg you, do not leave me alone wiz Petair. 'E is so sweet, but such a leetle boy. 'E think 'e love me. 'E think I love 'im.' Then with classical French simplicity she pulled a face and said 'Merde!' She then started to put on her coat.

It was at that moment I knew all my doubts and suspicions about Peter and Sophia had substance. I remembered so clearly Peter shaking his head in disbelief that day on the set. 'It can't be true. It just can't be true.' And of course it wasn't. Peter had set some sort of record in marital relationship. To go back to your wife and, unprompted, confess to genuine infidelity could be called eccentric. To go back and confess to infidelity that had never, in fact, ever taken place was almost beyond belief.

CHAPTER EIGHT

THE PINK PANTHER REARS ITS LOVELY HEAD

That old cliché about 'having a pound for every time' would have made a fortune for me if it applied to phone calls from Peter. With Anne and the children gone, he was living alone in the Hampstead flat and seemed to spend most of his time on the telephone. It must have helped with the depression. But the call he gave me one day certainly wasn't depressed. 'Guess what,' he started off. This, by the way, was his favourite opening with me. It invariably meant he had an amazing new gadget, or car, that would make me call him a lucky bugger. He got such delight from possessing things that would make him, if only for a little while, the envy of others. It really wasn't any form of conceit or greed. You calling him a lucky bugger verified, in his mind, that he'd made the right decision in the first place by acquiring that selfsame object. He liked to be reassured.

This call wasn't about property. This call was about money which, strangely enough, he hardly ever discussed. 'Guess what,' he said. 'I'm going to Rome, for five weeks, working for a director called Blake Edwards, in a film called

The Pink Panther, and guess what?' The repeat of this line was my cue. 'What?' I said.

His diction was very clear and precise. 'They are paying me eighty thousand pounds. For just five weeks!'

Well I didn't call him Golden Bollocks, or lucky bugger. I think I probably just said 'Christ!' Such a sum was beyond our comprehension, and gave Peter the first inkling of just what it could be like out there in the international marketplace. The next few minutes were a joy. 'Got any idea how much a week that is?' he went on. I realized why he said that. Translating any amount into a weekly sum always manages to get it into perspective. 'Well, let me see,' I said. 'Five into eight goes ... I'd better get a pencil.'

Mathematics was never my strong line and Peter wasn't too gifted that way either. Out came the pencil (no pocket calculators then) and, after a lot of feverish calculations, I finally worked out not only the weekly, but the daily amount. 'You do know,' I said, 'presuming you are working a six-day week, which on a location film could be normal practice, that you will be receiving two thousand six hundred and sixty-six pounds, sixty-six pence recurring, a day.'

Off to Rome Pete went, filming *The Pink Panther*, and off to Spain I went, filming a pilot for American TV, *Man of the World*. Then, two months later, in July of 1962, we were together again on an Elstree aerodrome making *Wrong Arm of the Law*, directed by Cliff Owen. I wasn't too happy about my film in Spain, but Peter seemed quite pleased about what he'd done in Rome. The glamour of shooting with Claudia Cardinale, David Niven, Capucine and Robert Wagner had obviously given him a lift, making *Wrong Arm of the Law* was almost like old times. Peter loved working with people he knew and the picture was full of performers he'd appeared with before. After the depression of the past few months he seemed to be taking on a new lease of life and my chief memories of the film are of long, sunny days on Denham aerodrome sitting side by side in deckchairs with Pete, Lionel Jeffries, and Bernard Cribbins, idly filling in time between scenes. That is until Cliff Owen had his brain wave.

'You *can* ride a motor bike, can't you?' he said. The interesting way the question was asked, implying that if I couldn't what was I doing on the film in the first place, naturally got the reflex answer that all actors give when asked if they are capable of any action from riding a horse to swimming fifty feet under water. 'Course I can,' I said. That grey, rather than white, lie nearly put paid to my friend Peter Sellers.

Sod's law applied to all forms of transport that appear in films. I've never driven a car in a movie yet that didn't have a slipping clutch, and if you ride in a carriage, even money one of the wheels falls off. Shown the large, black, 500cc Matchless twin motor bike I felt concerned. Told I would also have a pillion passenger I felt suicidal. The only slight light at the end of the tunnel was the fact that the passenger was to be Davy Kaye, who was not only a very funny comedian, he was also very small.

With all five foot of him mounted behind me I set off on a few practice runs. As we were at an aerodrome there was nothing to stop me driving about and I got quite confident. Peter sat in his deckchair, loving every look of terror on Davy's face as we drove up and down. Then came the take.

'I want the bike coming straight towards camera,' said Cliff Owen, 'and I want you to pass by it as close as you can.' He then suddenly shouted 'Action!' Well, he got the bike coming towards him, he got us close to the camera, and he certainly got action. 500cc of motor roared as I kicked into gear, let in the clutch, revved up the engine and, with a sublime look of confidence, drove straight at Peter's chair. Sod's law was working overtime as the adept turn of the wrist on the throttle control hadn't the slightest effect. It had, of course, stuck. Peter gave a yell and did a kamikaze leap out of the chair, Davy dug his fingers into my shoulders and threw himself sideways, and I wrenched the steering as far as I could. We missed the chair by inches and the bike finally juddered to a stop. Cliff Owen gave me an old fashioned look. 'All this motor-bike driving you did in the past,' he said, 'I presume was going round the Wall of Death.'

I also sensed that things were getting back to normal with Pete as new cars started appearing once more. That was always a good sign. To help in the spiritual recovery, we had a visit from the wonderful gentleman who had walked Peter and me down Park Avenue in New York wearing his bowler hat. Julie Munshin, with lady, was in London and he was as funny and delightful as ever. We did our best to repay his hospitality by showing him some of our sights. Since the weather was so lovely, Pete decided we should take him and his girlfriend on a traditional English picnic. Just a quiet, peaceful picnic. We should have known better.

The meeting place was our house and the four of us waited for Pete to arrive. Dead on time, the largest, most beautiful, brand-new, metallic beige Rolls-Royce convertible drew up outside our door. Happily sitting in this glorious conveyance, with the roof down, was Pete. He gave Julie, myself, and our two ladies a beaming smile. 'Well,' he said, 'you can't go out for a picnic without an open car.' Not many people would buy a Rolls-Royce specially to go picnicking in, but Pete had. And that wasn't all. The boot was filled with the largest hamper Fortnum and Mason's had in stock as well as a set of folding seats and table.

Lounging back in the Rolls, as if this was an everyday occurrence, we glided away past every enviously twitching net curtain as Peter, paraphrasing Leslie Charteris, pointed the long nose of the Rolls north. Up Barnet Hill, left at the Norman Church, through Arkley, past the Thatched Barn, the scenery getting more and more rural. It was England at its most glorious. The tarmac wound on and on while our stomachs were getting emptier and emptier. Peter was glorying in his new Rolls, the rest of us were thinking about food.

'Maybe down that little lane?' Julie suggested. Pete was in one of his there'll-be-something-better-round-the-corner moods, so on we drove, but the crew were getting mutinous. 'I may start biting into the leather seats any moment now,' said Julie. Pete gave a scowl and brought the car to a sudden stop. 'Very well then. We'll eat on that piece of grass there.' The hamper was unloaded and unpacked, the table and seats were set up and, while startled drivers drove round and round us, we sat and solemnly had our picnic on a grass roundabout on the A1.

* * *

Later that year the first screening of *The Pink Panther* took place. It was in the small Twentieth Century-Fox preview theatre in Soho Square, which was always a favourite as it had an elegance which many of the preview theatres in Wardour Street lacked. I knew when Pete asked me to go to the screening with him that he was very nervous. Something about working with, or for, Americans seemed to put him on edge.

The audience comprised some of the cast—David Niven was there—plus most of the film crew. Peter introduced me to Henry Mancini who'd composed the music for the film. The small theatre was packed and some of the audience had to make do with the floor, but nobody cared. From the start it was a winner. The theme tune by Mancini was funny and delightful, the film looked gorgeous, the women divine, Niven more elegant than ever, and Peter walked away with the movie. Inspector Clouseau was his finest hour. It was so original, it was so real, it was so pathetic but, most of all, it was so funny.

We walked back across the square to the car, Peter continually giving me the glances I knew so well. Furtive, worried, questioning. Then he couldn't stand it any more. 'Was it all right?' he blurted out.

I stopped and looked at him. 'Well, all I can

say is, I've never seen anyone steal a picture like that before.'

The film was a monster hit and was a turning point in Peter's career. Copying his accent became a national pastime, and in Hollywood they were down on their knees thanking the Great Producer In The Sky for sending them this Oh-So-Multi-Talented English Actor. A sequel was obviously just a script away.

★ ★ ★

In the meantime, Pete was contracted to make a film in New York, *The World of Henry Orient*. Before he left I'd opened in *The Bed Sitting Room* with Spike Milligan in the West End so the call from Pete came through to the stage door. 'Any chance of you coming to the flat tomorrow? Rather important.'

When I got there he explained he was putting all the furniture in storage while he was away. 'However,' he said, pushing open a door. 'What about this lot?' This lot seemed to be the entire contents of a camera and hi-fi shop. It was wall-to-wall equipment, filling almost all the room and was, of course, the best money could buy. (Peter always shopped on the elementary principle that, if it was the most expensive, then it had to be the most efficient.) 'Right,' he said 'I want you to have all this.'

Even I knew that wasn't quite what he had in

mind, but of course with Peter you never could tell. 'Can't trust all this in storage,' he explained. 'They're bound to damage it. You're the camera expert, and you know a lot about hi-fi. You look after it for me. It's all insured and naturally you can use whatever you like.'

After a quick inventory of what was there I hired a medium-sized van and, at dead of night, so no one would realize just what I had stored in my modest home, I backed the truck into the garage, and hid all the equipment away. You couldn't really blame my stealth as the insured value was over eighteen thousand pounds, and this was twenty-five years ago.

For weeks I lived in a state of sheer joy. Any picture I wanted to take, there was the camera. Any piece of music I wanted to hear (mono, stereo, quadraphonic) was mine at the press of a button. I could have made my own sound movie if I'd wanted. Then one day I had a brain wave. 'I think I'll play a joke on Pete,' I said. Audrey got that maddening look on her face that implied that, while women have managed to grow up, men were still schoolboys, but nevertheless I persevered. Every bit of equipment Peter owned came out of the boxes. It took hours to lay it all out, but finally I set the delayed action on the Linhof camera and took a picture of myself, lying like some potentate amongst all the gleaming chrome. I sent a print to New York, writing underneath it, 'You don't think you're going to get any of this back, do you?'

A week later a large envelope arrived from New York. In it there was a photograph of Peter, reclining in the same position as myself, surrounded not by cameras and hi-fi. Oh no. For his photograph he'd persuaded several Miss World girls (in New York for the contest) to drape themselves around him. Underneath the picture he'd written 'Who the bloody hell cares!'

I could have killed him.

Audrey gave birth to our first son, Christopher, on 8 August 1963 and I realized how my status in life had changed when one of the nurses at the London Clinic, watching me nurse my son for the first time, gave me a knowing smile and said 'Proved yourself now, haven't you!' This proof of manhood came at just the right moment as five days later I walked on a set ready to appear in the film *Becket* with Richard Burton. The nurse may have built up my ego but Burton took it down a peg when he saw me dressed in monk's robes with my hair cut in pudding-basin style. 'Oh God,' he said with a grin, 'I didn't think it was going to be that sort of picture!' I loftily assured him that this was a dramatic role—as the Pope's secretary—but spoiled the effect by scurrying across the set in my first scene with my long robes sweeping the floor, rather like a religious hovercraft. Burton's laughter that day was on a par with Peter's giggles.

* * *

Peter sailed back from America with Blake Edwards. The sea voyage was to give Blake time to complete the script of *A Shot in the Dark* which was to be the first full starring vehicle for Inspector Clouseau. During the voyage Blake decided that Clouseau should have an assistant, Hercule, and Peter suggested me. Blake looked blank so *Spotlight*, the casting directors' bible, was produced.

Very democratically, regardless of status, *Spotlight* gives each actor, or actress, an equal half-page. You have a photograph, and written underneath, your height, the colour of your eyes, and the address and phone number of your agent. When it comes to the photograph, a great deal of heart searching goes on. In this particular edition of *Spotlight* my picture was one, taken on a recent film, of me as a French gendarme. I chose it because I thought I looked rather dashing in the hat. It also served as an introduction to a director that, up to date, I've made eight films for. Blake took one look at an actor already dressed for the part, and the contract for me to play Hercule arrived the next week.

Sadly, they've now pulled down the MGM

studios at Elstree but in November of 1963, when we started shooting *A Shot in the Dark* there, it still had its big, successful, Hollywood in England feel about it. On its stages, I got my first initiation into filming with Blake Edwards. The atmosphere was relaxed, with none of the pressure I'd been used to in the past. No 'Well, we haven't got time for that' or 'I don't think we ought to hold up for a laugh there'. Blake was one of those directors who never imposed himself on an actor. You were always invited to contribute what you liked to a scene, providing it was funny.

From Inspector Clouseau's first entrance, when he and Hercule drive to the murder scene, and he steps out of the police car, going headlong into the ornamental pond, it was laughs all the way. The character Clouseau expanded easily into being a star in his own right, and it was in this picture that the legend of Peter and the giggles was born. It started when I returned, as Hercule, to the office, and Peter spun a huge world globe, catching his arm in it. Peter ad libbed a line about Africa being all over his hand and we both started laughing. I've got a video of the film and I sometimes play that scene back in slow motion so I can still catch the start of the grins on our faces just before the editor put in a quick fade.

The best example of the relaxed atmosphere on the film was when we came to a scripted line which merely said 'synchronize watches'. Blake gave a smile and suddenly said, 'Who decides what time you synchronize to?' Pete and I laughed, then Blake said, 'Make it up without rehearsal. Action!' Sure enough we completely ad libbed that scene in one take, and it became a high spot of the movie.

Maybe it was because Louis B. Mayer, the founder of the studio, had a say in its design that the MGM restaurant was one of the best. He might have been a monster, but he was famous for always seeing that actors had somewhere good to eat. The best-quality chicken soup was always available. This was a tribute to his mother, who brought him up on it. Though we didn't necessarily have the chicken soup, Peter and I lunched there every day. Always the restaurant was full of famous stars like David Niven, Gregory Peck, Shirley MacLaine. Every table had its roster of film fame. Pete and I became blasé. We saw them every day and while familiarity didn't exactly breed contempt, it did take a bit of the gilt off the gingerbread. After all, a film actor is a film actor. Then one day Chester Morris walked in.

Pete and I did a triple-take. Chester Morris, one of the idols of our childhood, hero of a dozen matinées at the local fleapit. He'd been the star of *Boston Blackie*, a B picture series of the mid-thirties, and his tough, broken-nosed, private eye character was one of our generation's greatest heroes. Emerging from the darkened cinema into the daylight we would blink our way down the street play-acting Boston Blackie, pressing our noses to one side with a forefinger, imitating that prizefighter's face, while threatening other members of the gang with 'Now listen, youse guys.' And here he was in person. Playing quite a minor part in a picture at the studio he sat modestly at a small table in the corner, away from the star-studded tables. Our shadows made him look up. He immediately recognized Peter from his huge success in *The Pink Panther* and stood up, giving a courteous, but rather bewildered smile. Peter gave a nervous cough and said, 'Do you think we could have your autograph?'

On the *Shot in the Dark* set we were spoilt. Permanently standing there was a huge billiard table, and nearby a grand piano. At the same time as potting a few reds you could listen to the urbane George Sanders, co-starring in the film, play classical music to concert standard, as well as singing in an opera-quality voice. He lived up to his sophisticated image by being very private, and seemingly self-controlled, but that exterior hid someone just as prone to mild hysterics as Peter. He was also rather careful with his money.

The penultimate scene of the movie, in which Clouseau attempts to unmask the villain, had the entire cast, with the exception of me, who was lurking in the cellar, sitting in the drawing room while Peter fell over every bit of furniture, trod on most of the ladies' feet, and had a conversation with George Sanders about Elke Sommer getting a 'Burmp' upon her head. Then their discussion about the 'murths' flying out of the cupboard. Vainly Saunders assured Peter they were 'moths'. Peter agreed. That was what he'd just said, 'Murths'. Saunders's mouth started to twitch, and a vein in Peter's temple throbbed as they both tried to control their laughter. It was a Friday, mid-afternoon, and Blake wanted to get the shot out of the way so he could make a fresh start Monday. Things got steadily worse until Blake pulled out a thick roll of money from his pocket and put it by the camera. 'Right,' he said, 'The next guy who laughs doubles that, and it's beer money for the crew.' Everybody but the actors cheered.

In the next take Peter went almost at once. Blake didn't hesitate. 'That's going to cost you eighty pounds,' he said. His eyes moist with laughter Peter looked at Bert Mortimer, his driver and general factotum, and someone who was never known to be at a loss, no matter what the circumstances. He pulled out the money and put it on the pile. It suddenly dawned on the crew that a booze-up of gigantic proportions was in the offing. The clapper board was just about to go in for the next take when Peter gave a strangled cry, clutched Blake, and half sobbing said, 'Right, I'll double the money again but you'll have to do it Monday.' He'd just caught a glimpse of George Sanders, carefully studying his face in a mirror, rehearsing not to laugh. George had suddenly realized that if he laughed next he'd have to put his hand in his pocket and, as far as George was concerned, £160 was no laughing matter. It was then Blake decided to cut his losses. They shot the scene on Monday. That film was twelve weeks of absolute bliss.

In a long scene, early in the picture, Peter kept telling me 'We must have the facts Hercule. We must have the facts!' Months later, after *Shot in the Dark* had been released—proving to be a huge box office smash—I stepped into a taxi, gave directions and settled back in my seat. The cab driver gave me a grin and said, 'I got the facts Hercule!' He then explained the line had been picked up by London cabbies and used whenever they asked their bases for information, or talked to each other on their two-way radios.

* * *

Earning every penny of his ten per cent my agent, Dennis Selinger, got me another film, *Guns at Batasi*, which was to start shooting at Pinewood Studios only two weeks after the final day on *Shot in the Dark*. A tough army drama, shot in documentary style black and white, it was a total contrast to the Panther. Dickie Attenborough headed a cast which included Flora Robson, John Leyton and a new girl from Sweden, Britt Ekland. Seven days before we started the picture I got one of the famous offhand calls, this time from the Oliver Messel suite at the Dorchester. Pete was waiting for his new house at Elstead to be ready and was slumming it in Park Lane. 'Doing anything special tomorrow?' he asked. I checked the diary—Wednesday 19 February 1964—and told him there was nothing special, and why? 'Well I'm getting married,' he said, 'and I was wondering if you'd come down to Guildford and be my joint best man with Dave Lodge.' I asked him if it was anyone I knew and he said no, but I was going to be filming with her next week.

Audrey and I had a two-hour drive to the Guildford registrar's office which half Fleet Street had under siege. We fought our way through the horde and found a very pretty, very self-possessed, blonde girl, in an elegant dress and petalled hat. I introduced myself: 'I'm going to be one of your best men.' (Evidently Dave and I filled the Swedish tradition of having two gentlemen to stand up for the bridegroom.) 'That will be nice.' It was Britt Ekland, speaking in that curiously overcorrect English that Scandinavians have. She formally shook hands, smiled sweetly, told the officials, 'We simply *must* have more flowers.' As they tried to meet this request, Dave and I got either side of Pete and Britt, ready to do our duty. The couple both said their 'I do's' and then we went outside to find that the other half of Fleet Street had arrived.

With the aid of the police, we battled our way back to Pete's new house at Elstead for the reception. It had just as much land as Chipperfield but, instead of Elizabethan grandeur, it was more rustic Walt Disney, with the kind of low-timbered beams that kept Elastoplast in business. Fortunately the wall surrounding the property was a high one as all the three thousand people outside it seemed to feel that they personally should have been invited to the reception. On top of this high wall perched the usual phalanx of press photographers, willing to risk their lives rather than risk the wrath of their editors by not getting some shots of Britt and Peter.

The inside of the house was packed with family and friends. Wanting some fresh air I went out through the french windows and heard a desperate cry. 'Gra!' The abbreviation made me realize it was someone I knew and sure enough there was Terry O'Neill, then just a pressman, now one of the top photographers in Britain, clinging for dear life to the top of the wall. 'For Gawd's sake do us a favour. We've got to get a shot of the bride and groom!' I went inside and convinced Pete it was only fair, and he and Britt went out and faced the press. She jumped up into his arms, and dozens of camera motor drives went off like machine-guns. Terry looked down and said, 'I owe you, Gra. I'll never forget.' And he never has done. When he knew I was writing this book he went to enormous trouble to see I got an actual print of the photograph he took that day.

We munched our way through a magnificent smorgasbord, especially brought down from London by Mario of Mario & Franco (two of London's greatest restaurateurs) then drank the conventional champagne, toasting Peter and Britt as they stood by the opulent five-tier wedding cake. Each tier, decorated with silver horseshoes, was apparently, owing to a cunning arrangement of struts, suspended in mid-air. Later that evening we all drove up to London where we had another feast, again especially prepared by Mario, this time at his Tiberia restaurant. Audrey and I sat opposite Peter and Britt, who sat at his left side. On his right was Peg. She looked very tiny, very old and, still not taking her eyes off Peter, sat with a frozen smile on her lips. But the look in her eyes said it all. She was rid of Anne but now had to face the replacement, and I don't think it was a happy moment. Britt dealt with her brilliantly. She oozed charm, but I think Peg realized this was an adversary not to be treated lightly.

That weekend Peter flew off to Hollywood to start shooting *Kiss me, Stupid*, written and directed by the legendary Billy Wilder. The following Monday morning, only six days after the wedding, the bride and the two best men reported for work on *Guns at Batasi* at Pinewood. Dave Lodge and I were playing two English sergeants in an African regiment, and were to spend the next eight weeks carefully seeing we didn't dirty our splendid all-white uniforms. Britt played a Swedish United Nations worker who falls in love with another sergeant in the regiment, John Layton. John Guillermin, our director, was very clever but could be tetchy. Britt didn't have an easy time as her English made it difficult for her to always understand what was wanted, and Guillermin found it difficult to communicate. During that first week's shooting there were some very tense moments and when we walked on the set the following Monday morning the folding chair, with Britt's name on the back, was ominously empty.

The next day Britt was cuddling up to Peter in his rented house in Los Angeles. The press had a field day. Screaming banner headlines told the world SWEDISH BRIDE FLEES COUNTRY TO BE WITH BRIDEGROOM. Inches of maudlin sob-sister columns went on about BRITT FLIES TO HER MAN. And they didn't miss out on the sexual titillation either. Every breakfast table in the country was made livelier by the implication that Peter's love life came before his wife's career. Then more headline news that Peter and Britt were to be sued by the film company for half a million pounds.

* * *

The *Guns at Batasi* film shut down for two days, then a very young, very long-haired girl came timidly on the set. She'd been flown in from New York to replace Britt. Taking over a part is one of the most difficult tasks known to an actor or actress so we crowded round to greet her and make her feel at home. 'Hello,' I said. 'I was in love with your mother.' She gave a laugh. 'All the men tell me that.' Her mother was Maureen O'Sullivan, who enchanted my generation as Johnny Weissmuller's mate Jane in the Tarzan films. The young girl's name was Mia Farrow.

CHAPTER NINE

HE CALLED ME DARLING ALL NIGHT

The reaction to Peter and Britt's behaviour was very different on either side of the Atlantic. In Britain, he had the advantage of being a native of the Isle. Far from harming Peter the Britt escapade gave him even greater fame. The thought that Peter had found, and made his own, the lovely Swedish nymphet—for that was how Britt was always portrayed—made him the envy of a large proportion of the British male population. In many people's eyes he became a 'bit of a lad', a tribute peculiar to his homeland.

In America of course it was a different matter. The Americans have a very deep-seated conservatism about show business. They do expect you there on time, you should know your words and, most important of all, you should never knock the product. Every one of these rules Peter and Britt had broken.

Guns at Batasi progressed. Dickie Attenborough, as a ferocious but fair-minded regimental sergeant-major, was giving the performance of his life. Mia Farrow was charming everybody on the film, and Dame Flora Robson, despite her age, had every man in the cast anxious to sit with her at lunch. We all adored her and one day, without thinking, I called her a dolly bird. She rose from her seat, came round the table, and gave me a kiss. 'I've never been called a dolly bird before,' she said, 'and I rather liked it.' She was a joy. Dave Lodge and I kept in touch with Pete, letting him know all was well in the old country, and passing on what gossip there was.

Filming for Peter in Los Angeles, unlike us at Pinewood, was not going well. The expected delight of filming with Billy Wilder was a giant let-down. Peter's basic dislike of Americans welled to the surface and things got very abrasive. Wilder liked working with an open set, anyone could wander on at will, and it drove Peter mad. I can't say I blame him. Being relaxed is one thing. Being the focus of casual onlookers is another.

There was certainly a strictly closed set at Pinewood on the day when a nude Shirley Eaton was being painted all over with gold paint in the new Bond film *Goldfinger*. Dressed in my crisp, spotless white uniform (the wardrobe department made sure we had a clean one every day) I sat alone at a small table having lunch, when Sean Connery, the ultimate James Bond, pulled the other chair away from the table and said, 'All right if I join you for lunch?' Over the meal he leaned close and said, 'You know it's Shirley Eaton and the gold paint today? You want to bring your camera over to the set. You could get yourself a great picture.' I didn't take the camera, as I knew a closed set prohibits it, but I accepted the invitation and after lunch there we were, Sean and I, sitting on two small chairs, in a tiny caravan, watching Shirley being gilded from head to foot.

In fact, Shirley wasn't actually nude under the paint. Two small corn plasters and a strategically placed strip of Elastoplast had been applied but the effect was just the same. At three o'clock I stood up as I had to be back on my set. As I said goodbye I had an inspiration. 'Give me a farewell hug,' I said.

Shirley cottoned on at once, gave a naughty grin, wrapped her arms around me tight, then gave me a big squeeze. When she stepped back, there, all over my lovely white uniform, were blotches of gold where she had pressed herself. Even my shoulder blades had the marks of her hands. Slowly, so as not to jar the effect, I walked back to our set and carefully placed myself just behind the camera. It was only a question of time before Dickie Attenborough, in the middle of filming a splendid speech, caught sight of me. Normally the most disciplined of actors, Dickie took one look, burst out laughing and said, 'Oh you rotten bastard!'

Apart from being hugged by almost naked gold painted ladies I was also getting the reflected glory of the enormous publicity engendered by Britt and Peter's marriage. It was the era of au pair girls and they flocked to England to assist in the running of our homes. A young girl from Italy, with the unlikely name of Emma, was one of our better ones. She very happily looked after the children, flicked a feather duster round the house, and ate her food with gusto. Well-built in the Italian manner, she seemed content until one day, giving me a fixed stare, and in her heavy Italian accent, she asked me, 'Ees right you were the best man for Peeter Sellers and Breet Ekland?' I told her yes. She digested this for a little while and then said, 'Ow long Breet Ekland in England before she meet Peeter Sellers?' The news that it was only a matter of days brought a slight gleam to her eye. 'And now she ees a feelm star, yes?' I gave a nod, and left it at that.

Two nights later I told her my agent Dennis Selinger was coming to dinner. 'What ees agent?' she said. 'Ees like a pradoocer?'

Once more taking the easy route I gave a nod. 'Just like a pradoocer,' I said, thereby nearly sealing Dennis's fate.

All through dinner that night, wearing clothes several sizes smaller than she usually wore, plus perfume that hit you at ten feet, Emma was a sensation. Constantly leaning provocatively across the table so that Dennis could get a better view of her ample cleavage she gave him the full treatment. Leaving the house, Dennis looked at me, almost accusingly. 'I never knew you had an au pair who looked like that before,' he said.

I gave a slight shake of the head. 'Until tonight neither did I.'

Fortunately for Dennis, she became enamoured of a small bearded youth and, giving up all thoughts of film stardom, vanished into the wilds of Tufnell Park, never to be heard of again.

* * *

Then on 7 April 1964 came the terrible news. In the space of only a few hours Peter, still in Los Angeles, had been stricken with no less than eight consecutive heart attacks. If there was publicity about Peter's marriage, and the subsequent flight of Britt, it was nothing to the bulletins that the radio, the television and the newspapers then put out. The time difference meant that we got the news mid-afternoon and I arrived back from the studio and sat watching the news bulletins on TV. The announcer's faces got more sombre as the evening wore on. It was horrific until I got the phone call.

A breathy lady asked if this was Graham Stark speaking. I told her yes, and she said she was calling on behalf of Rediffusion TV. 'I feel I must tell you—' the tones were now hushed and reverent—'that according to our latest information your dear, *dear* friend Peter Seller's life is drawing, very, very gently to its close.' If only she hadn't stressed the second 'dear' so much, and had not used 'very' twice. 'I think,' she went on, the breathing getting quite dramatic, 'you must be prepared for the . . . [in the pause we got a little extra gasp] . . . loss of your closest friend.' Even more was to come. 'We have a car standing by and we would appreciate it if you would come to the studio and record a eulogy about him.'

I felt the occasion warranted an equally hushed tone. 'If it's all the same to you,' I said, 'I'd just as soon wait until he's actually dead;' and reverently put the phone down. I'd tried all the way through the conversation to concentrate on what she was saying but all I could see was an image of Peter's face laughing when I told him about it. Somehow I was convinced I would tell him, and therefore I wasn't a bit surprised when I suddenly read he was sitting up in bed wanting to know what the fuss was all about.

Peter loved comic phrases and one of his favourites came out of a story Dave Lodge told about himself. With his marvellous physique, Dave didn't get grovelling parts, he got muscular parts. While working on a Viking action film, *The Long Ships*, he was leaping about wearing just a horned helmet and enough strategically placed fur to get by the censor.

Dave had posed dramatically in front of camera, his muscles rippling. 'As my body was lightly oiled at the time,' Dave said, 'the effect was terrific.' From that moment on 'lightly oiled' became part of our private language.

Still working on *Batasi* at Pinewood, and determined to give Peter a laugh I got hold of a large brown bottle and labelled it 'LIGHT OIL'. Dave then stripped down to his singlet and the studio photographer took a picture of me apparently pouring the oil over Dave, and sent a print off to Peter. He told us later that when he saw it he laughed so much he nearly had another heart attack.

*   *   *

In June Peter and Britt returned to England and moved back into Elstead. The film company dropped the lawsuit against them but, as always, Pete couldn't resist a dig at Hollywood. He said what he thought was true about being on public display while working there, and all hell broke loose. A telegram from Wilder, Dean Martin, and Kim Novak, accusing him of being disloyal to his fellow artists, made every front page. The accumulation of news stories—first about his marriage, then about Britt's flight to America, followed by his near death, and now the telegram scandal—gave Peter more publicity in three months than most actors would have in their lifetime. Out of all this adversity Peter emerged a world-wide household word. The legend was now established. His eccentricity, his waywardness, even the great lover image, all combined to make his every move and every word reportable.

The invitation to Elstead came as soon as he was back, and Audrey and I drove the road to Guildford once more. We went down a country lane, over a hump-backed bridge, then, like a jack in the box, we saw Peter shoot up from behind a hedge. He went about twelve feet up in the air, then dropped back out of sight. My tyres squealed as I stopped the car dead. Peter shot up from behind the hedge again. He was wearing a jump-suit and looked very happy. 'Hallo Gra, hello, Aug,' he gasped then disappeared behind the hedge. Audrey and I were like two nodding puppets, our heads worked by a string, as we carried on this extraordinary conversation. Each time Peter bounced up, he spoke. 'Got to do this.' BOUNCE 'Doctors say it's—' BOUNCE—'good for the—' BOUNCE—'heart. Anyway I'll be—' BOUNCE—'finished soon. Go and—' BOUNCE—'see Britt.' All was explained as we drove through the wrought-iron gates. There was Pete, under doctor's orders, serenely bouncing up and down on a trampoline.

Picking up where you left off has never been

a problem with actors. Separated for ten years they'll meet in the street and practically carry on the conversation they were in the middle of the last time they met. Everyone knows just what everyone else is doing and, if you've any doubts, the newspapers and television will be only to happy to tell you. The who-is-married-to-whom file is very carefully kept up to date and, most important of all, the cast of every show is carefully tabulated just in case one of them drops dead and you might be right for the part.

Meeting up with Peter after all that had happened was a perfect example. He knew you knew, and you knew he knew you knew. The mid-air conversation had magically broken the ice and Britt helped by obviously being glad to see us. Pink and panting from the trampoline, Pete flopped back on the settee. 'Oh Christ, it's great to be home. Soon as we've had the tea I'll show you round the place. Having a lot done.' If I'd thought I was going to see a frail Peter, just recovering from several major heart attacks, I was totally wrong. If anything he was more active. He looked great, with a much slimmer figure, and an enthusiasm for life that I hadn't seen for a long time.

Pointedly, he never referred to the time he'd spent in hospital. He seemed possessed with a euphoria, realizing he'd been given the ultimate second chance, but something told me this was not the time to call him Golden Bollocks. In fact I never called him it again. In future times, when professionally he became so difficult, I always reminded myself that Peter was living on borrowed time.

We went for a tramp round the grounds, and I admired the area where the horses would be stabled, and was shown where the new six-car garage was going to be built, the one with the cinema on top. Half of Guildford heard a section of the latest Mantovani LP, as Pete demonstrated what he assured me was the ultimate hi-fi, and cunningly I got out of driving the new motorized lawn mower by saying I'd prefer to look at the two new cameras he'd bought. In other words, things were back just as they used to be. Admittedly he'd changed the house, and his wife, but apart from that I couldn't see any difference.

* * *

The phone calls were just as regular, and although Elstead was that much further away we still managed to get down to see Peter and Britt. Every so often he'd come to us and on one of those visits he broke the news that Britt was pregnant. Naturally we had to celebrate, so once more the flight to Paris for the four of us and, without the slightest hesitation, Peter booked us once more into the Raphael. We ate at the same restaurants, and Pete and I tried to be very brave while Britt and Audrey did the Paris shops. We had such great memories of times in Paris with Pete and Anne, but with Britt it was great fun too as she had her own delightful sense of humour. In retrospect, I've always thought Britt had rather a bad press. I can only say I always found her funny, entertaining, and very kind to Michael and Sarah (Peter's children by Anne). It seems that people can't equate glamour with being a nice girl. Wear a slit skirt and you're a marked woman.

The next dramatic phone call was all about instruction books. As I've already said, Pete couldn't tolerate them. 'Gra,' the voice was quite desperate, 'you and Aug have got to come down tomorrow; stay to dinner of course. I've rented this film projector but I can't make the bleeding thing work. By the way, it'll be roast beef.' As a dinner invitation it was, at least, original.

A heavily pregnant Britt opened the door and Pete showed me the very large, gleaming 16mm sound projector that stood at the end of the room. 'None of that hopeful button pushing,' I told him, and started reading the instruction book. A reel of film was already on the front spindle. 'Home movie,' said Peter. 'Couple of friends coming over after dinner to see it.'

It was one of those Under No Circumstances

instruction books so I read it through twice. The electrics were easy, the threading of the film was a bugger. It writhed through the projector like a berserk snake with puncture holes along each side. Each hole had to fit every sprocket precisely, and heaven help you, according to the book, if you didn't make your loops correctly. Well, after twenty minutes of cursing, my loops were in beautiful shape and everything was fine. Britt and Audrey made appreciative noises while Peter, alias Major Bludnuk, told me I was a white man.

After dinner I was standing in front of the fire drinking my coffee and warming my rear end, when the 'couple of friends coming over after dinner to see it' walked in. Wearing a rather smart cocktail dress and looking smaller in real life than in her pictures, Princess Margaret came up beside me, rubbed her hands in front of the blaze then, in a clear, high voice said, 'You know, I always laugh when I see you come down the hill and get that boxing glove in the face.' She was of course referring to *The Running, Jumping and Standing Still Film*.

'Ah, you've seen the film then,' I said, stating the obvious.

'We,' she said, warming her hands some more, 'have our own copy.' At first I thought she was using the Royal prerogative, but then I realized she was indicating her husband, Lord Snowdon. He came over, shook hands, and told me that Peter had in fact given them a print of the film and it was their favourite viewing. Then we started the game of musical chairs, getting ready for the screening.

Peter got the settee, with Britt and Audrey either side of him, while Margaret and Snowdon, delightfully democratic, perched on a couple of stools. I switched on the projector, hoping to God I'd got my loops right, then sat down on another stool in between Margaret and Snowdon and waited for the film to start. Even though it was a home movie of Peter's, and only in black and white, it was 16mm and had sound. As the film began I laughed as Peter appeared as Fred Thrump, lightning-quick-change artiste, doing terrible impressions of various celebrities. We got Tod Slaughter as the Demon Barber of Fleet Street, a bit of Lon Chaney as the Hunchback of Notre-Dame, then Fred Thrump looked straight at camera. 'I will now do,' he announced, 'in what I can safely say is the world record time of six and one quarter seconds, my celebrated impression of Her Royal Highness Princess Margaret.'

He dived behind the Victorian screen that stood behind him, hurried music played as clothes were flung over the top then, to my absolute amazement, instead of Fred Thrump, Princess Margaret popped out from behind the screen. She waggled her hips like a conjuror's assistant, blew a big kiss to the camera, then dived back behind the screen. Almost at once Peter, as Fred Thrump, shot out from the other side. He looked at an old-fashioned gold turnip watch in his hand, then at the camera. 'I just broke the record,' he said. 'This time I done it in six seconds.'

Pete had proved once more that in the realms of gamesmanship he was a master. Only he would have the nerve to get a member of the Royal family, the sister of the Queen, to play stooge to him in a comedy film. But there was more to come. Peter then did another sequence, with himself and Snowdon as a couple of gangsters discussing ways of killing another mobster, which was absolutely marvellous. 'You gonna put his nose in the light socket and switch on the light?' Pete's accent was wonderful. Snowdon shook his head. 'How about his feet in a bucket of cement, and into the East river?' Once again Snowdon silently shook his head. 'If it's not the light switch, and it's not the East river, how are you goin' kill him?' Snowdon gave a great pause, dropped a limp wrist, and with a sibilant accent said 'That's *entirely* my concern.' After fifteen minutes the film ended with a finale in which Princess Margaret, Peter and Snowdon did a high stepping chorus line singing the Gang Show signature tune 'Riding Along on the Crest of a Wave'.

Then the lights clicked on, after the most

exclusive Royal Film Performance I'll ever attend. To my delight Margaret turned to me and, with her precise diction, said, 'Oh, I do feel such a fool. Me, such an amateur, being watched by all you professionals.'

And that was the moment I came nearest to getting my knighthood. 'Don't worry,' I told her, 'you were great. You should have been an actress.'

Pete phoned the next day dying to know what I thought. I told him we'd had a great evening and that his film should get an Oscar nomination for the best supporting cast of the decadc. Then Peter said, 'You made a hit yourself last night with HRH. She called this morning to thank me for the screening and told me she did like that Graham Stark.' Pete laughed. 'Evidently you called her darling all evening and she loved it.'

CHAPTER TEN

INSPECTOR CLOUSEAU MEETS CITIZEN KANE?

As if personally taking on nature as an adversary Peter seemed to ignore totally the fact that he had been so ill. Obviously he had to obey his doctors, but nevertheless he was subscribing to a pet theory of mine that lying gracefully on a chaise-longue with the vapours is not the way to recuperate. Just after my marriage in 1959 I was recovering in hospital from some minor surgery when Peter and Anne came to visit and found me, one arm hooked through a chain hanging from a frame above the bed, busy making plastic models. Within minutes Peter was aiding and abetting me when in walked Professor Fleming, the surgeon who had peformed my operation. Tall and elegant, with long slim hands, he peered over half-moon glasses at Peter and me who, like two schoolboys, were assembling a model train. A small gaggle of young doctors behind him hung on his every word. I was having a tricky time getting the wheels on and, as Pete was already holding the front bogie, passed the boiler house to Mr Fleming. 'Hang on to that while I get some glue on the axles,' he said.

Mr Fleming took the boiler house in those elegant hands, and beamed at the young doctors, who in turn were delighted to see their most senior surgeon assisting Peter Sellers and Graham Stark in the making of a model train. 'Now you see gentlemen,' Professor Fleming explained, 'this patient will make a very quick recovery, for the simple reason he's much too busy to be ill.' And he was right. Normally after such an operation, I should've been using crutches for six months. In fact, after three months, I was in a West End revue doing complicated dance routines every night.

Peter's therapy didn't take the form of complicated dance routines, it took the form of a Superfast Ferrari capable of doing 160 miles per hour. You might have thought that after the heart attacks he would have settled for a sedate town carriage, but that wasn't his way. The gleaming monster car—specially imported—stood in the six-car garage. It was Peter's pride and joy . . . just like all the other seventy or eighty cars he'd owned in the past.

He sat behind the steering wheel, caressing it. 'This is the one, Gra. This is the car for me.' As I'd heard that several dozen times before I didn't take a lot of notice, but I did take notice of the giant surge as, with a roar, the car took off. If I'd had a mirror I'm sure I'd have seen my face flatten out like that of an astronaut being trained on a centrifugal machine. The acceleration was beyond belief.

Away we went down those narrow winding lanes that you only find in the English countryside, and the high hedges either side gave the effect of hurtling down a narrow green tunnel. He must have looked at the dashboard. 'Look at that,' he cried. I wasn't able to look at anything as by now I had my eyes tight shut. 'Eighty-five and I'm not even in top,' he went on. I took his word for it and suddenly became very religious, assuring God that if only I got out of this alive I would dedicate the rest of my life to good works. Luckily nothing came out of any side turning, and finally we drew to a standstill. With relief, and a fair amount of trembling, I climbed out of the car.

We both had cameras with us that day. Peter his new Leica, me my Hasselblad, and soon we were busy taking photographs of each other.

* * *

Then two baby girls were born within five months of each other. The first was Kate Levy, daughter to Anne and Ted, who appeared on 17th August 1964. The second was Peter and Britt's daughter, Victoria Sellers, who arrived, by chance, on my birthday, 20 January 1965. Audrey and I naturally went to admire the baby and congratulate Britt. I made a lot of cooing noises, which the baby very sensibly ignored, while Audrey took out a new pound note, made it into a tight roll and checked if the baby would grip it. Just as sensibly, Victoria grabbed it and held on to it. Britt laughed. 'I wish all our friends were like you.'

The baby boom reminded Audrey and me it was time for our son Christopher to be christened. Combining a small amount of diplomacy and a large amount of cunning I asked Audrey's agent, Walter Jokel, to be one godfather, and my agent, Dennis Selinger, to be the other, working on the simple principle they would both try even harder to make sure their godchild's parents were kcpt fully employed. Apart from which they were very nice men. Within days of this arrangement being settled Peter was on the phone. 'Can he have three?' he said. I assured Pete that, as far as I knew, there were no restrictions re numbers so now Christopher had three godfathers all of whom dutifully turned up at St Barnabas's Chapel on 27 December 1964

It was Peter who introduced me to the Reverend John Hester., Rector of St Anne's in Soho, who performed the christening, and it was an introduction to someone who became a close personal friend and also a person who was to be very close to Peter right up to the very end. That Sunday morning we crowded round the font. The lady who 'did' for us, Mrs Hurlin, was godmother and the three godfathers noted with relief that she was the one who held the baby while the ceremony took place and bless him, Christopher never cried once. He still has the ornate, beautifully inscribed silver mug Peter had had specially made to celebrate the occasion.

* * *

Nineteen-sixty-five was also the year that two films were made that greatly affected both Peter and me. In London I was working by the Thames with a young cockney actor in a picture that was to be a landmark in his career and, in a smaller way, didn't do me any harm either. The actor was Michael Caine, and the film was *Alfie*. Michael made an enormous hit, the film grossed a fortune, and every member of the cast, including myself, gained prestige just by being in it.

In Paris, alongside the Seine, Peter was wearing a manic black wig, speaking in a mid-European accent and being, as always, very funny in *What's New Pussycat*? This was also a huge hit and put Peter right back in business. He proved he was still box office. The industry, as the film world likes to call itself, instantly forgot the heart attacks, instantly forgot problems of health insurance, and queued up once more to offer him work.

Head of the queue was Charles Feldman,

who'd produced *Pussycat* and was delirious not only about the success of the film but also by the contribution Peter had made. He returned that with interest as Peter turned up at my house one day, driving a beautiful new Rolls-Royce. I did the usual admiring walk round it, had the obligatory test drive (luckily I didn't have to check any squeaks in the boot, or speed down any country lanes), and was then told that Feldman had given the car to Peter as an end-of-picture present. It was a pity I'd decided never to call him Golden Bollocks ever again, as it would have been just the right phrase to use at that precise moment.

Feldman also gave Peter the chance to play in a James Bond film—and what actor could turn that down? Feldman owned the rights to *Casino Royale* and planned to make a frenetic, episodic comedy of it, with an all-star cast. In the first sequence of the picture, Peter was to play an accountant by the name of Tremble called in to beat the villainous Le Chiffre (played by Orson Welles) at the gaming tables. It all sounded absolutely marvellous, and turned out to be a disaster of titanic proportions.

The film started shooting mid-January 1966, directed by Joe McGrath, at Shepperton Studios, with an enormous budget, huge sets, and a script that apparently was being written ten minutes before each scene was being shot. As it was such a colourful film Peter told me that any time I wanted to take my camera onto the set I could. So one day I went to Shepperton and found the rumours about the film being in a mess were untrue: shambles would have been a better word. The huge gambling casino set was bedlam, and hundreds of extras, in expensive clothes, milled aimlessly about. A young man kept appearing from a caravan waving a piece of flimsy paper in his hand on which, I gathered, the script for that morning's work had just been written. Even worse, this was the day the dramatic gambling scene with Peter and Orson Welles was to take place.

One of the great legendary figures of Hollywood was about to meet, on screen, the most spectacular new comedy talent of the decade. Well, that was the original idea. But it was not to be. Peter, for reasons best known to himself, retreated like a snail into a hard shell of non-co-operation. Steadfastly he flatly refused to appear in the same scene as Orson Welles, even though the climax to the whole casino sequence was their confrontation across the gaming table. Basically a very funny idea, it featured Peter as Tremble, the accountant with a computer-like brain versus the malevolent Le Chiffre, played by Welles, whose only answer to his opponent's mental wizardry was to go into a bravura conjuring act.

Unbelievably, Peter never even came on the set while Welles was present. He sat very tight-lipped in his dressing room, looking alarmingly thin, and extremely unhappy. It is a tragedy that Peter never shot the sequence with Welles—it would have been quite something to watch—but he seemed to be in the grip of superstition that was controlling him more and more. Welles, according to Peter, had some sort of evil aura. Joe McGrath, the director, whom I knew well from television, tried to look brave, but was obviously feeling the strain. The only serene person seemed to be Welles himself.

Already a huge man, he looked even bigger dressed in a white tuxedo. From his mouth jutted a cigar that made one of Lord Grade's Havanas look like a cheroot. He sat at one of the gaming tables, a slight smile on his face, and pointedly played patience while all around him technicians worked out elaborate camera angles that were to cover up the fact that, although Welles was supposedly in the middle of a tense and dramatic duel of wills with a man on the other side of the table, the man on the other side of the table was staying in his dressing room.

As if he wasn't gifted with enough talent, watching Welles flip the cards of the pack, placing them in neat alternate lines of suits, reminded you that he was also an accomplished magician. His hands were incredibly supple, and as each hand of patience ended, he couldn't resist some card manipulation, enjoying the oohs and aahs from the twenty-five beautiful girls cast as Le Chiffre's personal entourage.

At least they managed to shoot Welles doing his magic tricks on his side of the table and it was something to see the man who made what is now accepted as the best film ever made, *Citizen Kane*, sit there, like a joyous schoolboy, producing flags of all nations apparently from out of the air, bouquets of flowers from his sleeves, and raising a horizontal girl up into the air without visible means of support. I was only sorry Peter wasn't there to enjoy it like the rest of us.

During a break in shooting I sat talking to Tracy Reed, who was on the picture—a lovely actress whom I'd worked with on *Shot in the Dark*. Her father, Sir Carol Reed, had directed Welles in one of his greatest successes, *The Third Man*, and Welles gave a smile when he recognized her. Slowly he strolled over to where Tracy and I were sitting and joined us at our table. I sat and listened to that awe-inspiring voice. 'You know something—' his gaze took us both in—'I could make an entire film for what this goddam scene is costing.' Right at that moment the young man with the flimsies appeared, handed Welles one of the now famous bits of script, and gave a smirk. 'I think you're going to love this, Orson,' he said. 'It's *terribly* you.' He then moved on. There was no pause in Welles's movements as he took the sheet of paper, crumpled it into a tight ball, and threw it over his shoulder. The cigar was back in his mouth and the lit end described an arc as he slowly shook his head. 'God save us from amateurs,' he said.

I was never originally in the picture but out of the blue, I got a call from my agent telling me the producer, Charlie Feldman, had personally called and asked whether I was free to go back to Shepperton that Friday, talk to Joe McGrath, and work out some scenes I could play with Peter. If something was worked out, Mr Feldman was suggesting a fee that was going to take care of my income tax for the year.

Once more at Shepperton, Joe briefly explained that Pete was hoping I'd join the picture and do 'something' with him to give the sequence a lift as it really wasn't going that well. It was straight out of *Alice in Wonderland*. 'Don't worry,' Joe assured me. 'You start Monday and we'll have something written for you when you get here.'

My agent arranged the deal with Feldman, I arrived Monday, and an American came up and shook my hand. 'Great to work with you, Graham. I'm Bob Parrish and I'm directing the picture.' Over the weekend Joe McGrath had been taken off the film and Bob Parrish had been flown in to replace him. During these few words I saw the young man make yet another entrance from the caravan, waving yet another flimsy piece of paper on which he'd obviously just been typing. 'This could be hysterical,' he said, then, as if to absolutely settle matters added, 'And Peter and Graham are *bound* to add some funny bits.'

The lunatics had taken over the asylum. From then on it was all down hill. We did our flimsy paper scene and tried to add some 'funny bits'. Being his first day, Bob Parrish, a delightful man, did his best, but did it rather carefully. He was going through a minefield and well he knew it. Broken glass was strewn everywhere and from that moment on everyone was going to do their best to tip-toe through it.

I was quite happy as I was preoccupied in working out how to take some photographs of Ursula Andress, and who could blame me? Her part in the film required her to wear an outfit that the adjective 'sensational' was designed for. The long evening dress was dove grey, the trimming was arctic fox, and the cleavage went as far as the censor would allow. She looked glorious. She was also a very charming lady, until I brought up the matter of me taking her photograph. 'That would be vairy nice,' she said, with all the enthusiasm of a comatose shop dummy. But Peter saved the day. 'You want to let Gra take your picture, Urst,' he said. 'He really knows what he's up to.' On that cue I produced the Hasselblad and took some pictures.

A couple of days later, while she was waiting for a shot with Peter, I gave Ursula a set of 12 x 10 prints. She was delighted but felt she owed an explanation of her reluctance to pose. 'The trouble is, wiz my teets.' Both Peter and I told her she had nothing to worry about in that direction but she insisted. 'The trouble is definitely weez my teets. You notice I am wearing a low-cut dress, yes?' We assured her we had not been looking in that direction, but now she'd come to mention it, yes we had been aware of it. 'I bend ovair to put out a cigarette like so—' she demonstrated—'and you see 'ow my dress falls away from my body, yes?'

Pete nodded. 'Gra and I see exactly what you mean.'

Now Ursula dramatically acted out the whole story. 'Ovair zere' her finger pointed into the middle distance—''eez a naughty photographer, hiding behind the scenery. Thees naughty photographer 'e 'as the lonk lens.'

Pete looked baffled. 'Long lens,' I translated.

'Thees feelthy swine,' Ursula went on, ''e wait until I bend ovair, then cleek, 'e takes the snap. I open some magazine and there, in ze middle page, are my teets.'

* * *

Like a giant paper-towel dispenser the caravan kept pouring out more and more sheets of flimsy paper, but very little actually got filmed. The entire gambling sequence ended like a damp squib, and unfortunately the film as a whole wasn't much better.

The powers that be in Hollywood, like most people faced with catastrophe, and desperately looking for a scapegoat, fell on Peter like wolves. He was, almost exclusively, blamed for the failure of *Casino Royale*, and what a failure it was. Committing every sin possible where glamorous comedy was concerned, the film was over-long, episodic, and extremely hard to follow. There wasn't a lot to be said for any of it. The fault, though, lay in its original 'wouldn't it be great to have a movie filled with stars and let's worry about the script later and by the way we'll have four different directors' concept. Peter was, after all, only in the first sequence, but nevertheless his refusal to work with Welles didn't help. If only someone had had the sense to have a showdown.

Unfortunately the star system in feature films has one great trap in which it's only too easy to fall. If you raise money on an actor's name, and they know it, it gives them a weapon. Before you even start they're in a position to manoeuvre for director approval, for script approval, and if they're not mad about the colour of the dressing room curtains you've got trouble there as well. It's even worse once the star has started filming. If confrontation comes they only have to threaten non-appearance and the producer is a spent force. He can't afford to reshoot and has to make sure his stars' every whim is catered for to make sure they continue to work.

Many never abuse the system, but Peter was always a law unto himself and would exert pressure, in any way he could to get what he thought was right. Unfortunately, in *Casino Royale*, just for once, his instincts were wrong. He tried to play Tremble as a normal, sane man, and secretly I think he saw himself as a pastiche of James Bond himself. Dieting down to a slim, almost thin, figure, he used a cultivated accent and made no attempt at comedy characterization at all.

In truth he really should have been playing the part Welles had been given, Le Chiffre's. He could have given it that strange lunatic quality that always lurked under the surface of his best performances. It wasn't a coincidence that almost all his successes were with characters that were, in themselves, unbalanced: Kite, the trade union leader, obsessed with exactitude; Clouseau the walking disaster zone, while Clare Quilty in *Lolita* and Dr Strangelove himself were both certifiable. Even Dr Pratt, using kittens as blotters, had a magnificent Dickensian madness. Playing the part of Tremble as an ordinary man was Peter's own choice, and photographs of him in the part show someone trying desperately hard to discharge himself from the beard, whiskers and false nose brigade.

CHAPTER ELEVEN

IF YOU WANTED LAUREL AND HARDY . . . ?

I realized, quite early in our relationship, that being any sort of yesman with Peter was fatal. Paradoxically the more you stood up for yourself the more he thought of you. This became clear during the brief time I once owned him. Well, to be strictly correct, during the time Dave Lodge and I jointly owned Peter. Once his income soared, Bill Wills, his financial adviser, asked Dave and me as two of Peter's closest friends, if, as a favour, we would sign papers, thereby becoming directors of a holding company. All Peter's income would be assigned to this company (helping his tax situation), thus Dave and I would, theoretically, be in possession of that income. I travelled to the city one morning and, with the smell of parchment and sealing wax in our nostrils, Dave and I signed where indicated. 'Right,' said Dave and I to Pete. 'You realize we shall now pocket the lot.' The three of us fell about laughing. The lawyers never even smiled.

Almost six months later, very early one morning, there was a phone call. The voice was male, adenoidal and rather rude. 'Are you

Stark?' it demanded.

I wasn't going to make the adolescent joke: 'No, I'm in my pyjamas;' so I merely told him I was.

'Be in Mr Wills's office by three o'clock,' Adenoids said. 'We need your signature to cancel the service agreement.' He then rang off.

I then called Bill Wills. I can't quite remember the words I used but they were to the effect that, if you did a friend a favour by signing an agreement, thereby saving him a considerable amount of money, the least the friend could do, if he wished the agreement to be cancelled, was to personally ring and ask you to arrange a suitable time to cancel the agreement that had saved the friend all the said money. I finished up, rather grandly, by stating, 'I am not to be summoned at will.'

The last phrase was a bit over the top but it seemed to do the trick. The next day a very contrite Peter rang. 'Sorry about that, Gra,' he said. We arranged a suitable time, I signed the cancellation form, and the matter was never mentioned again.

* * *

Late in 1966, we were both off to 'foreign parts'. Actually Peter went to Rome to film his own production of *The Bobo* with Britt as his leading lady, while I travelled just down the road to Pinewood studios, where they'd built a Spanish village on the back lot. There I spent several happy weeks playing one of the two comedy villains who were trying to do down heroic Cliff Richard in the film *Finders Keepers*. The other villain was the bumbling, eccentric, corpulent, joyous personality who goes under the name of Robert Morley. We may not have had the sun and heat of Rome but, by all accounts, we had a far happier time.

Once again Peter made a fatal error. Bob Parrish, who'd taken over on *Casino Royale*, was made director of *The Bobo*, in which Peter played a strictly minor leaguc Spanish matador. Parrish was a gentleman in the full sense of the word, with a great record as a cutter, and a director, but, when it came to in-fighting, he was no match for Peter. As it was Peter's own production Bob had no option but to let him have his own way (Peter wanted, but was not permitted, co-director credit on the film) and the picture suffered for it. It was so strange that for someone with the most impeccable built-in taste when it came to acting, Peter's overall view of a film could be disastrous.

Producers, directors, friends, fellow actors, all tried to advise him against these self-damaging decisions, but what could they do? With the track record he had you couldn't put up much of an argument. The only thing you could wish for Peter was someone who could match his will power. It wasn't a coincidence that the only film he made at this time that was any kind of success was *The Party*, directed by Blake Edwards, one of the few directors who seemed able to keep Peter under control.

* * *

Peter's mother Peg died on 30 January 1967. She was seventy-two. He was still in Rome when it happened. Her death slid him just a bit further down the slope of gloom. Nothing seemed to be going well and his phone calls got more plaintive and sad. He took to lighting a candle to the memory of Peg and once more the spiritualists and fortune tellers saw their chance and moved back in. We had a few laughs at Elstead, and I dutifully admired the new cars. They changed so often the garage began to look like a dealer's showroom, and I carefully managed to avoid any test drives as one of them was a Lamborghini, and other an E-type Jaguar.

One day I got another call about working the projector. This time I didn't get to see Princess Margaret in a home movie, but I did see a marvellous comedy made by American director Mel Brooks. The picture was *The Producers*. Peter and I sat at Elstead, tears running down our faces, as we saw this marvellously original comedy with two sensational performances by Zero Mostel and Gene Wilder. Peter had originally seen the picture in Hollywood and thought it was so brilliant that he actually paid for an advertising campaign which quoted him as saying 'This is the funniest film I've ever seen.' The print I watched with him was given to him in gratitude by Mel Brooks as Peter's efforts eventually made it a big hit. Years later I met Mel Brooks and he admitted he owed his career to Peter's generosity.

* * *

In mid-1968 Pete and I lost a friend. Tony Hancock, alone in a hotel room in Australia, took some pills, washed them down with his last glass of vodka, and finally ended the awful descent from the wonderful heights of comedy he'd achieved. For me it was a sad, tragic ending to someone who, many years before, had been almost as close to me as Peter. I've always remembered with affection how he rescued me from that dreadful basement room in Holland Park. I remembered too a funny young airman of twenty-two, who used to have tea with his mother and me in the Regent Palace Hotel whenever she came to visit London. Surreptitiously she would always slip a five-pound note under the table to him. The tragic note found in the room after his death, in which he had written, 'Things seemed to go wrong too many times' was addressed to her.

Tony's marriage had ended only a few days before he took his own life and that news added to Pete's now acute depression. His marriage to Britt had started to show signs of wear and tear. Late in 1968 the divorce came through. By fortunate coincidence, finance also came through for his latest project, *The Magic Christian*, which typically, he decided should be directed by Joe McGrath whom he'd had unceremoniously removed from *Casino Royale*.

Peter had his own, quite extraordinary, rules regarding the people he worked with. He could have someone taken off a film, but only if he believed that that someone was wrong for the job. He could then go to a lot of trouble to make sure he worked with that person again because this time he sincerely believed that person was right for the job.

The Magic Christian, in reality, never had a chance. The final sequence where Peter, as a cynical millionaire, watches as the greedy public willingly swim in excreta to earn money, wasn't what that same public wanted to see. Peter managed to assemble a very good cast, including Ringo Starr playing his son, plus cameo roles by Raquel Welch, Roman Polanski, Yul Brynner and most of Peter's favourite fellow character actors including me. Happily dropping back into a grovelling role as a waiter,

I was working out a comedy routine with Joe McGrath and Peter when there was a bit of a flurry at the back of the set. At Peter's invitation Princess Margaret had come to watch the filming. Unfortunately, she'd picked a bad day. The set was small and crowded and, royalty or no royalty, filming had to continue. Somehow they fixed a seat near the camera for HRH while we got on with the job.

I had thought of quite a funny piece of business which entailed my fawning for a large tip by bowing low then, still bent double, leaving the scene by walking out backwards. 'Great,' said Joe McGrath. 'Let's just make sure no one's in Graham's way when he backs out to camera.'

Princess Margaret gave a delighted cry. 'I'll see no one's in his way. I really will!' And with a splendid imperious wave of the royal hand, she cleared all round her, then gave a reassuring nod. On that signal the clapper board went in, the camera announced he had the right speed, Joe McGrath called action and, with the same abandon as I had showed at Denham on the motor bike, I walked out backwards—straight into Princess Margaret's lap. There was a big laugh from the crew, a squeal of delight from her, and I climbed off her lap with as much dignity as I could. As I turned to face her she gave a big smile and then said, 'We've met before. Do you remember?' Temptation swept over me. With a poker face I was all set to say, 'Now, don't tell me. The face is familiar, but ...?' Then suddenly I had a vision of being rowed, full tilt, through Traitors' Gate while they dusted off the block in the Bloody Tower. I politely said, 'Of course I do,' and even remembered not to call her 'darling.'

It really was a bizarre film. In one sequence there were fifty topless girls, meant to be galley slaves, being whipped into action by Raquel Welch. They sat in rows at their oars while Peter and I watched with delight as the chief make up man Harry Frampton (a highly moral gentleman) had to go to each girl and spray her breasts with body make-up as the camera man was complaining of too much flare.

* * *

It was the summer of 1969 and Audrey and I had just moved into our new house as we now had our second baby, our daughter Julia. We spent every spare moment putting right the damage the great British workman had inflicted on our property at what they assured us was a very reasonable price. Nine o'clock one evening I was balanced on top of a stepladder when the phone in the hall rang. The voice was deep, mid-European and said, 'Pliz, to Graham Stark I would like to speak.' I gave a laugh. 'Very good, Pete,' I said. 'But if you don't mind, I'm fixing a bleeding light bulb.'

The voice didn't alter. 'You haff a light bulb that bleeds? And who iss Pete? You theenk perhaps I am Peeter Sellers?' He laughed.

'Yes I bloody well do,' I said. 'And I'm going back up that ladder.'

The voice got quite urgent. 'No pleez. Am Gene Gutowski, prodoocer for Roman Polanski. Am not Peeter Sellers, but am calling *about* Peeter Sellers.'

Then I realized it really *was* Gene Gutowski who *did* produce for Roman Polanski. I made the usual excuses and he understood: 'I know Peeter well. Also know is possible he could play me better than I could.' He thought this very funny, laughed for a while, then got down to business. And what lovely business it was. Peter had really done me proud this time.

Gutowski explained that Peter had agreed to play a cameo role in a film Roman Polanski had written, *A Day at the Beach*, and was going to produce in Copenhagen. A young Moroccan protégé of Roman's, called Simon Hersera, would be directing. Peter would be playing one of two rather faded effeminate gentlemen in a beach bar. Now came the big bit. 'Peeter is not charging for beeing in feelm. Peeter is doing feelm for free.' Try as he could he couldn't keep the delight out of his voice. 'However,' and now there was just a note of uncertainty, 'Peeter only play part in feelm if you play other part.'

The uncertainty vanished and was replaced by straighforward pleading, 'You like play old queen?'

I assured Gutowski I would love to play old queen, and the next day my delighted agent told me Paramount was going to pay me a lot of money to fly to Copenhagen in just under a month. This time it was me calling Peter. 'You', I said, 'are a Prince among men. How did you know I always wanted to go to Copenhagen?'

Peter gave a laugh. 'Because you're a filthy swine like me!'

A week later I was sitting in a dentist's chair, in Barnet Village, with three people grouped tightly round me—the dental surgeon in white coat, his lady assistant in white coat, and Roman Polanski wearing black leather and a wicked grin. 'Upper left incisor gold,' said the dentist, pushing hard. 'Upper left incisor gold,' noted the assistant on a pad. Roman just said, 'That make you look even more like a queen.' The little demon genius was a known fanatic for detail and had decided that a couple of flashing gold caps on my teeth were just what my character needed. Roman stepped back to admire. 'You and Peēter are going to be beautiful in this feelm.' My reflection in the mirror did nothing for me, but who could argue with Roman Polanski. Luckily the two gold caps were sent on ahead as I didn't think I could face Peter on the plane with heliograph signals flashing every time I opened my mouth.

Eagerly Pete and I gazed down as the plane came in low over Copenhagen airport. In those days, the late 60's, it was known as the naughty city of Europe and there were stories of hordes of young, long-legged, unbelievably glamorous, blonde girls, smoking joints of marijuana, and living a life of free love. As far as the floor of the King Frederic hotel goes all that was true. The film company had taken it over and, as Peter and I stepped out of the lift, the smell of pot hit us like a solid wall. Down the corridor, arms open wide in greeting, came two Poles (Roman and Gene) and one Moroccan (Simon). Each had *two* of those long-legged blondes in tow. I looked at Pete. 'Are we going to be terribly British?' I said. Pete grinned back. 'You can do what you like. I think I'm going native.'

We got the obligatory bear hugs, we were shown our rooms, and then the party started. After that we had one every night. The news that Peter Sellers was in town was on every front page of every newspaper in Copenhagen coupled, rather meaningfully, with the news that he was now no longer married to his Swedish wife Britt Ekland. The effect was, to say the least, alarming. After all, hadn't my friend already shown a liking for ladies Scandinavian? The *femmes fatales* in the hotel lobby were a sight to see. There was no actual accidental dropping of handkerchiefs or bumping into him as he came out of the lift, but it wasn't far short of that. One day we went out for some publicity shots by the Little Mermaid and it was almost Beatles at London airport time. And then there were the all-night barbecues on the beach. The midnight sun was still in the sky when they began and I'd like to know where the myth of the gloomy Dane came from. We had a marvellous time, but there was a film to be made, and in a few days, after the clothes had been fitted, and the make-up set, we were at the studio ready to shoot.

I thought Peter looked quite fetching in his pale blue crew-necked sweater, a scarf loose round his throat, his hair curled and wearing slightly tinted oblong glasses. I looked outrageous with open-necked shirt, colourful scarf pulled into a gold ring, my hair combed forward Roman style and wearing enough jewellery to put Liberace to shame. The gold teeth gave just the right sibilance to the voice and I kept wondering if Peter and I would manage to get through the scene without laughing. Derek Cracknell, known as probably the best first assistant director in the world, checked out the set of the broken-down beach stall selling cheap novelties and souvenirs, which was run by the 'old queens', Peter and myself. Roman Polanski, as producer, was hovering, along with Gene Gutowski, but the man in charge was the director Simon Hersera. He was very young, very charming, but as soon as he opened his mouth I knew we had trouble.

Looking as bizarre as we did it should have been obvious we had to play against our appearance but Simon decided it should be a comedy scene with a capital C. He described what he wanted for a few moments, then Peter's chin went up, the eyes narrowed, and he said, 'If you wanted Laurel and Hardy why didn't you book them?' Nobody spoke. Simon looked at Roman, Roman looked at Gene, and Peter looked at me. Then, to my horror, he said, 'Come on, Gra, you know what you're talking about. You tell us what to do.'

Well, it's not every day you're asked to take over directing a film produced by Roman Polanski, especially when the official director, the producer, the executive producer, the first assistant and about forty members of the crew are all gathered around. It was not quite what I'd bargained for. Once again eyes started darting from face to face. I looked at Simon, who gave a nervous smile and looked at Roman, who looked at Gene, who backed out of the light and looked at his feet. Finally Roman looked at me. He gave a tiny shrug, a brief smile and, most important of all, a small nod. Peter, the only one quite unconcerned, gave an expectant smile in my direction. 'Well,' I said, tentatively, 'Peter could start over here and I can come through the beaded curtain ...' Gradually, the tension eased and soon we had the scene worked out. Simon followed the action with the camera, prompted, I'm quite sure, by Roman. At the end of the day we had at least got something filmed.

Gene and Roman were waiting in my dressing room when I got there. They both gave me the bear hug and, as an extra bonus, I got a kiss on each cheek. Gene was the spokesman. 'Roman and me were werry pleased the way you help today. Wizzout you ...!' He drew his hand dramatically across his throat. 'Also we both theenk you make helluva old queen!'

Roman and I were to meet up again a few weeks later on a historic night. Every year, without fail, my agent Dennis Selinger gave a party for his birthday, which became a social event. On the night of 20 July 1969, all his guests turned up at the River Club, owned by James Bond producer Harry Saltzman. That night it glittered with fairy lights, while outside the window, the River Thames rippled slowly by, bathed in romantic moonlight. Not that any of us at that party were remotely interested in our surroundings. We all stood, clutching our glasses, watching the huge television screen in the corner, hoping to God nothing would go wrong with the first Moon landing, that was taking place, live, before our very eyes. There was a roar as the crackly voice spoke of the giant step for mankind. The Man On The Moon was at last a reality. Typically, Michael Caine grinned at our host. 'I gotta say, Den, you did fix a nice cabaret.'

I bumped into Roman and we clinked glasses, then he took me by the elbow and led me across to a window seat where a young girl was sitting. Very blonde, very beautiful, and very pregnant. Roman introduced me. 'Ees Graham. Graham Stark. Veery 'elpful to me and Gene in Copenhagen. 'Ee make lovely old queen.' Then proudly he indicated the young girl. 'Thees is my wife, Sharon Tate.' The next morning they flew to Los Angeles and twenty days later her dreadful killing took place.

★ ★ ★

Early next year *The Day at the Beach* was given a private screening in London, to which Pete and I went, along with a few executives, and it was after that screening it was decided never to release the picture. It was very sad, mainly because of the remarkable performance by Beatie Edney, the daughter of Sylvia Syms. Now one of our most exciting young actresses, she was then an enchanting seven-year-old, who had just lost her milk teeth, and was a scene stealer the like of which I had never seen before. The sequence Peter and I had shot was quite funny in a wry way, but the overall effect of the film was so gloomy that you couldn't argue with Paramount's decision.

Fortunately for me there was a happy ending to our trip to Copenhagen. On the flight back I landed at London airport where I carried out a long-standing tradition, and thereby got the chance to direct Peter in a film for the second time.

CHAPTER TWELVE

'YOU,' SAID BRYAN FORBES, 'ARE A CHEEKY BUGGER.'

My eldest son Christopher, who was godson to Peter, and now a sturdy four-year-old, was following in his godfather's footsteps by being passionate about cars. This simply meant that every time I returned to the house from being away, his little face was alive with curiosity. What model car had Daddy bought? It says something for the amount of work I was doing at this time that his playroom table was covered with rows of exotic model cars. He went through a delirium of joy when he found the Chitty Chitty Bang Bang car had expanding wings, and soon it became obvious that the models had to do something, apart from just sitting there looking good. Coming off the plane from Copenhagen my prayers were answered when I saw, in a gift shop, the model of the Simon fire engine.

In the grown-up world the real machine was a Simon snorkel hydraulic hoist, nicknamed the Cherry Picker by all the film and television technicians that used it. It can be seen today at every television golf tournament, towering above the crowds like a spindly giraffe, a camera in its top basket. The model I bought was the fire engine version. It was bright, shiny red, had a few bits of silver on it, you could run it about the carpet and, most important of all, the tower with the fireman in it opened like a giant pair of scissors. It became Christopher's favourite toy. Up and down the carpet it went, with the tower fully erect, and, as I watched, I had one of those brain waves that don't come very often, but when they do, you know you've had a good one.

I scribbled a few notes and, after seeing the machines in action at Simon Engineering in Dudley, I sat down and wrote a script and was fast-talking Hemdale pictures into putting up the money for a short film. Then I persuaded the ACTT (the Association of Cinematograph Television and Allied Technicians) to let me have a temporary director's ticket, and finally there I was, assembling a cast. With very little money I got Julia Foster, Norman Rossington and John Junkin to join me in the venture, a debt I shall owe all three of them for ever. Then luck was on my side.

Michael Caine and I had become close friends after I'd worked with him on *Alfie*, and that very week I was meeting him for dinner. On the way to the restaurant I thought up a joke appearance for him. As I had so little money I worked out that at the beginning of the film, the title sequence was to feature me pasting up the names of the cast on already existing posters dotted around London. 'Go To Work On An Egg' became 'Go To Work On A John Junkin'. The Pan Am poster now read 'Julia Foster Makes the Going Greater.'

I told Michael I was going to paste Norman Rossington's name over his on a film poster. I wanted Michael then to ride by, in an open-topped Rolls-Royce, reacting with fury when he saw what I'd done. Michael burst out laughing and said, 'You're on!' After that came Morecambe and Wise, Bob Monkhouse, Bernie Winters, David Hemmings, Pete Murray, Tony Blackburn, all doing cameos and working for nothing, which proves yet again that actors' generosity to their fellow actors knows no bounds.

Peter made one of his frequent visits to the new house but for once he didn't arrive alone. This time he came to show off his newest lady friend, a Miss Minnie Bannister, spinster of this parish. She was in her early forties, with a body that had been completely renovated, and was still capable of giving a performance that, considering her age, was quite remarkable. Minnie was an imposing 1929 Austin motor car that Peter had lovingly restored to all its former glory and had named her after one of the most famous characters in *The Goon Show*, played by Spike Milligan. An aged spinster, with a quavery voice, always insisting 'we'll be murdered in our beds!', Minnie's name perfectly suited this lovely, ancient car. Christopher was given a ride and his face was filled with rapture as he was allowed to honk away on the large, rubber bulb that sounded the horn. As soon as Peter found about my film project he was as quick off the mark as Michael Caine had been and agreed to appear.

The face of John Daly, chairman of Hemdale, when he saw the cast was something to see. 'They've all agreed, for nothing!' His voice had the same slight tremble as Gene Gutowski's when he told me, 'Peeter is doing feelm for free.' Four weeks later we started shooting in a deserted fire station in North London, and the weather was on my side. I kept up to schedule. In the meantime Michael Caine had started filming *The Long Valley* in Germany, but he'd given his word and, like the gentleman he is, he flew back one Sunday afternoon, came to North London first thing Monday morning, did his scene for me, then got on the lunchtime plane and flew back to Germany. And that's what I call friendship.

Peter was also filming but he wasn't as far as Germany. He was just up the road at Elstree, but strangely enough his appearance presented just as many problems as if he had been abroad. In his picture, *Hoffman*, he was in virtually every scene and there was no morning or afternoon off, no matter what. We'd have to shoot him during his lunch hour. The joke I had for him was based on his well-known passion for cars. I wanted him to come out of the studio gates, in an elegant motor, be in an accident, then at once change from his car into another one just the same, but a different colour. It gave the impression of unlimited cars always at his disposal.

I went and saw Bryan Forbes, who was then head of the studio, and asked him if I could have the whole front of the studio without traffic, and with the gates wide open for one hour. Without hesitation he gave me full permission to shoot where I liked and agreed to stop all traffic. 'Regarding Peter,' he said. 'He can do what he likes in his lunchtime, but we've got to have him back prompt at two.' Prompt at one o'clock, all traffic ceased, the studio gates were opened and, to Peter's delight, he came out to find I'd managed to get two identical Lamborghini cars, one red, one blue. I think even Pete was impressed by that. We set the camera, I called action and Pete drove the blue Lamborghini out of the opened gate and a stunt car drove into his front end, damaging it. Peter leapt out, glared at the damage, snapped his fingers and at once the red Lamborghini was driven out to replace it. Without blinking, Pete got in and drove away. We covered it in a closer shot, Peter shook hands with my tiny crew, and went back in to have his lunch. Bryan Forbes was watching from his office window in the centre of the administration block. I waved a grateful thank you, and smiling he waved back. 'You,' he said, 'are a cheeky bugger.'

Luckily the film worked very well and a few weeks later I screened it for Peter, and the rest of the star-studded cast. Peter loved the film, especially his joke with the cars. We called the film *Simon, Simon* and it made a lot of money. For Hemdale that is, not for me. But who cared. That short film was a labour of love and it went on to my being asked to produce, and direct, a feature film, *The Magnificent Seven Deadly Sins*. This picture of course was in a different league and it wasn't something you could ask your friends to help you out with. Fees had to be paid, and we weren't in the position to afford Peter Sellers, but I did manage to sign the other two goons, Spike Milligan and Harry Secombe. Before shooting could begin, however, there was a formality.

Although the ACTT had issued me with a temporary director's ticket, before tackling a feature movie you had to have a full one. Les Wiles of the ACTT, who was in the position to grant the ticket (one of the most highly prized documents in the cinema business), told me there was one rule I had to obey. 'You've got to get three fully paid up fellow directors to sign your application form—and take my tip, the more important they are the better.'

Right, I thought, go for the best. Number one was easy. Ken Hughes had directed one of my favourite fantasy movies of all time, *Chitty Chitty Bang Bang*, and was an old friend. He signed at once. Peter, who of course had his own director's ticket, signed as number two. Letting the whole thing go to my head I decided Stanley Kubrick should be number three. He was on location near my house doing some night shooting on *A Clockwork Orange* so I drove up there. Derek Cracknell, first assistant on the film, nearly had a fit. 'You can't see Stanley now, Gra. He's rehearsing Malcolm McDowell, just the two of them. I daren't let you through.' God knows how I managed to get past him but I did.

At one end of a small, bare room was Malcolm wearing his bizarre costume and the terrifying boots which, in the film, he used to kick a victim to death, while he sang 'Singin' in the Rain'. At the other end of the room Stanley sat on the floor watching him through the eyepiece of a 16mm Arriflex camera. Without pause I moved in beside him, took out my application form, removed the camera from Stanley's hands, and asked him to sign on the dotted line. Malcolm's jaw dropped, Stanley was too bewildered to do anything but sign, and I shot back to London and the very next day presented the application form to Les Wiles. He took one look at it and said, 'Why didn't you get David Lean and Carol Reed while you were at it!'

If it was fun directing Peter in *Simon, Simon*, it was a joy to direct Harry Secombe in the *Seven Deadly Sins* picture. He was a professional's professional: the first on the set in the morning, absolutely word perfect, he would accept any kind of directing without a murmur. I watched Harry with fascination, for he was such an extraordinary contrast to Pete. They'd worked together for so many years in the Goons, were close friends, shared exactly the same sense of humour, were both talented performers, and yet in Harry was a contentment, and a joy in living, that Peter never seemed able to achieve. The answer of course was Myra.

Harry had married this delightful Welsh lady back in 1948, and their happy marriage has lasted to this day, Myra giving him the stabilizing influence that Peter had lost when he and Anne had parted. While they were still together Anne's laughter alone could bring Peter down to earth. Any sign of him starting to believe his own publicity was enough to give her the giggles.

Typical of Harry he adored telling the story of how, when he was making his first big movie, *Davy*, he relaxed one Sunday afternoon in front of the fire. As he was the star of the film, and was in almost every shot, he was glad of the chance to get a day off. He was stretching in luxury when Myra's pretty face came round the edge of the armchair, and in her delightful Welsh voice said, 'Come on, Gregory Peck, let's 'ave the coal scuttle filled, shall we!' Therein lies sanity.

But Peter did keep trying. He married Miranda Quarry on 24 August 1970. Stepdaughter of Lord Mancroft, Miranda was very sweet and charming, but I always felt her county background wasn't really Peter's scene. He was never comfortable with people from outside the theatrical profession, and in many ways Miranda's high intelligence and breeding acted against her where Peter was concerned.

The reception was at Tramps, the well known nitery, or, in this case, dayery. We were halfway through the lunch when Warren Beatty slipped into the chair beside me. 'I thought I was never going to make it. Just got off the plane from LA.' He looked round at the reception then leaned a little closer. 'Tell me something,' he said. 'Where's the action?' Now there was a single-mindedness one was forced to admire. Straight out of a taxi from London airport, he fortified his reputation as a ladies' man by immediately asking where the girls were. Why he thought I might know I never understood but I could see why Woody Allen, when asked if he believed reincarnation existed said, 'No, but if it does I'd like to come back as

Warren Beatty's fingertips.'

Nineteen-seventy was the year the whole world got excited about space travel. We'd seen man's foot crunching on the moon dust that night of Dennis Selinger's party, and the lunar traffic was building up to a steady flow. It was purely a matter of time until something went wrong and, sure enough, the whole world was suddenly riveted by the drama, the ultimate horror, of men trapped in a space ship, unable to get back to earth. Every front page carried the story, every radio and television newscast gave us the latest bulletin. Would they, or wouldn't they, make it back? With potentially the greatest television viewing audience the world has ever known it was announced that there would be live coverage, in colour, from an American aircraft carrier in the South Pacific of the dramatic re-entry of the space capsule.

At 5.45 in the afternoon (with events like this you always remember the time) I sat, transfixed, in front of the TV watching as the cameras scoured the skies, waiting for the first glimpse of the tiny capsule as it hurtled back to earth. The terse clipped voices of the astronauts were still coming through, but any moment now, when they went through the heat barrier, all vocal contact would be lost. For several minutes we would just have to wait, hoping they would appear.

It was precisely then that the phone rang.

Audrey was out so, compelled by the shrill call, I had to answer. I dived out into the hall and picked up the phone. I wasn't too polite. No giving of my phone number. I just snarled 'Yes!' The well-known voice seemed a bit far away but I could hear well enough. 'It's Peter,' it said. 'Are you watching the telly?'

Still with a terseness to the voice I said, 'I *was*.'

'Thank Gawd for that.' Pete's voice was filled with relief. 'I'm in Paris, the bloody TV in the hotel is on the blink; you've got to tell me what's going on with the astronauts.' Only Peter could make a trunk call from Paris to check what was on the TV. Unfortunately, my telephone lead was on the short side (no cordless phones then) so, to talk to Peter, and see the television at the same time, I had to lie on my side, on the hall carpet with my head wedged round the half-open door of the lounge. For twenty minutes I gave a running commentary on what was going on in the Pacific Ocean. Halfway through the call, Audrey came in through the front door and saw an apparently headless husband lying on the floor. I only had to call out 'Peter' and she understood at once. I daren't think what the call cost him, but bills never seemed to worry Pete. Which was probably why his accountants now suggested he become a tax exile in Ireland.

Peter's last few films had done very badly at

the box office, and for the first time in his life he really had to start worrying about money. He hated leaving London but financial pressures were brought to bear. In February 1971, just before he and Miranda went into their not so voluntary exile, they came to St Paul's Church, Covent Garden, where the joint christening of my two younger children, Julia and Timothy, was taking place. As always, John Hester (who'd played a very important part in Peter's convoluted religious life) was in charge. Brian Clarke, Eddy Braben and Christiana Kubrick were godparents to Timothy, while Peter and Miranda were godparents to Julia. It could have been the imminent exile to Ireland, but pictures taken that day show a sombre-faced Peter, dutifully cuddling Julia, wearing, as if in preparatory mourning, a long, black cloak.

The farewell party was at the San Lorenzo, Beauchamp Place on 25 March. One of the in-places for the show-business crowd, they did Peter proud. The restaurant was festooned with streamers and balloons, predominantly emerald green (they meant well but it was Peter's un-favourite colour), and the guest list had every newspaper photographer fighting for lens room on the pavement outside. It really was a Who's Who of the film world and society. They all came to see Peter off. He and Spike did a bit of comedy passing round the hat, making as good a joke as they could about the tax exile bit, and there was a lot of cliché putting-on of Irish accents. Princess Margaret and Lord Snowdon turned up, plus the brother and sister pair of Warren Beatty and Shirley MacLaine. As the room was filled with glamorous girls, Warren didn't need me this time to tell him where the action was. I had a wonderful time doing a frantic version of the twist with Joan Collins, who'd just agreed to join the cast of my *Seven Deadly Sins* film. She was a sensational dancer, as well as having a deliciously wicked sense of humour, and it was very sad that, purely for contractual reasons, she couldn't eventually make the picture with me. It was a great party but I only wish I hadn't kept getting the feeling we were all attending a bright, fun-loving wake.

* * *

While Peter was, fiscally, bogged down in Ireland, I was working like a maniac at Pinewood, finishing off my feature film. We'd got to the cutting-room stage when, in one of those extraordinary coincidences, my past with Peter came back with a vengeance. In its simplest terms the cutting of a film, when it's completed, means just that. The master negative remains untouched but you can cut prints, made from that negative, in any way you see fit, joining them together to form the film you want. Everything, with the aid of your editor, is straightforward until you come to any silent section of the movie. Then, for technical reasons, you have to run, on the sound side of the movieola, a piece of old, dud, film which the lab at the studio will supply at a set rate per footage. Normally the editing room has an ample supply, but as we had a long silent sequence, starring Spike Milligan, we soon ran out. The assistant editor went off to the film store, which stocks thousands of feet of old film, and brought back a can which he loaded into the movieola.

The editor and I were discussing a cut when the assistant called, 'Governor, I'm looking at you. You and your mate Sellers.' (Calling me 'Governor', by the way, is British film tradition. The director gets called that from the first day he walks on the set to the last day of the film.) Sure enough, on the viewer was a piece of film that had not felt the warmth of a projector lamp for over twenty years. A little movie that isn't even listed in Peter's film credits. Made in a basement studio, in Dean Street, it starred Peter, Dick Emery and me as three bowler-hatted idiot city gents involved in a complicated spy plot. The name of the epic was *Super Secret Service*, and that very piece of film is still with me to this day. It's black and white, with sound, and it's absolutely terrible. It is also a wonderful memento of the days when Peter and I were running about the West End, willing to work for fourpence providing it was a film.

I ran the film, then called Peter in Ireland and told him what I'd found. He was thrilled and spent half an hour on the phone reminiscing about what he called the good old days, which was in contrast to the bad new days he was clearly going through in the so-called Emerald Isle. Not that you could use that term with Peter. He had this fixation about green being his unlucky colour and certainly his time in Ireland must have fortified his view. His career at this stage was almost non-existent: financially he had got to the stage of having to borrow £5,000 to keep solvent, and emotionally he had patches of almost suicidal depression.

Fortunately, there were a few opportunities for him to get back to London, and we had a perfect example of his amazing resilience, and ability to bounce back when, on 30 April 1972, to help celebrate the fiftieth anniversary of the BBC, that venerable body mounted a programme that was utter anarchy. The venerators, the devotees, the lifetime fans, the Goon Show Preservation Society, plus the entire Royal Family, with the exception of the Queen and Prince Charles, all gathered at the Camden Palace Theatre for one of the most memorable broadcasts of the decade, *The Last Goon Show Of All*.

The publicity was extraordinary and it was a

media event. As well as the enormous radio audience that would hear the programme even BBC TV were going to be there to record visual highlights. The application for audience tickets became a torrent, and you could become a celebrity by casually mentioning that you were going to be there. I got tickets for two reasons. Firstly I'd been in many of the past shows, and the BBC are very loyal. Secondly, Max Geldray, who was being flown back from America to play that magical, swinging harmonica in the show once more, stayed as a guest in our house.

Like every other Goon Show in the past the recording was on a Sunday night, and while the outside broadcast BBC TV cameras panned across the audience, picking out the celebrities, the Fleet Street boys outside lit up the sky with their flashes as the Royal Family made their way up the red carpet to the foyer, and then to the front row of the dress circle. They may have got what is known as the posh seats, but we, the die-hard regulars, sat in our seats in the stalls ready to laugh as much as we'd done on those magic original recording nights years before.

The orchestra got a roar of applause. Then the announcer, Wallace Greenslade, followed by Max Geldray and singer Ray Ellington, got the same fantastic reception. Finally, from the wings, came Spike, Harry and Peter, and it was pandemonium. The three Goons revelled in the wall of noise that hit them. It was already an incredibly emotional night, and the show hadn't even started. Dismissing the twelve years that had passed since their last Goon Show together, they clowned round the stage as if the series had never ended, and blatantly incorporated the Royal Family in all their ad lib jokes. Peter peered down at the stalls through his now famous horn-rimmed glasses and, smiling benignly, called out, 'Hello, Anne darling. Hello, Britt darling;' and I had to admit, watching him standing there, totally relaxed, that Pete certainly had style. It's not every day you have two ex-wives in the audience, both smiling and waving at you, and manage to make it look like an everyday occurrence.

Just before the recording began, Wally Greenslade, in his very best BBC announcer's voice, read out a telegram from a sailor who was serving in foreign parts. The telegram voiced the despair of this sailor at not being present at the show, 'especially as my father and sister are both able to attend. My hair has turned green with envy,' it went on, 'and my knees have fallen off.' The telegram was signed, simply, Charles. Knowing that it was Prince Charles, currently serving on a destroyer in the Mediterranean, who had sent the wire the audience gave a huge laugh; then the recording started.

There was no anti-climax. The show was sensational. Possibly one of the greatest roars of laughter ever heard over British radio exploded after Peter uttered, in the voice of his character, Bluebottle, the immortal phrase. 'What is it, my Capitain!' After twelve years it went to prove the Goons never lost the love and affection of its audience and, verifying they'd really become the Royal jesters, Princess Anne was talked into recording horses' hoofs for them in the studio before the show by banging coconut shells together in front of the microphone.

The party in the bar upstairs, after the show, was just as big a success. You could tell that by the sheer volume of 'Darling You Were Wonderful' noises. Once again I heard that clear, high voice behind me: 'I say, wasn't the show absolutely super?' I turned and renewed my acquaintance with Princess Margaret once more. 'Absolutely super,' I said. She moved a bit closer and got quite conspiratorial. 'Do you think,' she half whispered, 'you might manage to introduce me to Max Geldray. I thought he was ever so good.' She was so delightful in her love, and awe, of show business people. I still think my reaction was right after seeing her in the film with Peter. She should have been an actress.

* * *

Near the end of that year, on 22 December, Audrey and I were the so-called guest celebrity pair on Bruce Forsyth's hit television show *The Generation Game*. The show always featured a pantomime-type sketch, which gave Bruce the chance to play parts with the contestants. Audrey and I were the talent judges. It was all harmless fun, and the show went well. Afterwards the BBC lashed out with few drinks, and the casting lady from Thames TV, Iris Frederick, gave me an arch smile and said, 'What do you think of my little daughter then?' She gestured to the girl who had played the heroine in the pantomime sketch. She was small, with enormous eyes and a tiny turned-up nose. Eagerly she pressed her forward. 'Her name's Lynne,' she said, 'Lynne Frederick. Perhaps you'll meet again some time. Who knows?'

CHAPTER THIRTEEN

ALLAH, ACHMED AND THE MOROCCAN ROPE TRICK

My experiences of Ireland have always been sheer delight. I always expected some anti-British feeling and never ever got any. Their accent, their story telling, their good manners enchanted me beyond words and it must be the only place in the world that at the end of a movie, where it's custom for a principal actor to give a present to his stand-in, I got a present from my stand-in instead. With all solemnity he presented me with a ticket for the Irish Sweepstake, telling me it had been a 'privilege and an honour to work with such a gentleman such as yourself'. It may have been blarney but it was such wonderful blarney. Sadly, none of that Irish charm seemed to have helped Peter in his stay there.

Apart from his brief triumph with *The Last Goon Show Of All*, when he did manage the odd day back in England one could see his face had taken on a more and more bewildered look, as if not quite understanding what was going on. The truth is that the two terrible all-powerful words 'track record', beloved by Hollywood, were beginning to have an effect. *Casino Royale* had done damage, the non-release of *A Day On the Beach* didn't help, a brief appearance in *Alice in Wonderland* hardly improved things, and finally the film he made in Jersey, *The Blockhouse*, about prisoners-of-war, also was never released. The effect on Peter's career became more and more apparent. 'I never did think he was that good' became the trite, flippant remark to throw in at a party. This was usually said by the same people who, a few years before, had breathed intense remarks like 'One doesn't want to use the word genius but . . . !'

At last back in London for a reasonable time, Pete invited me to a preview of a new photographic exhibition Tony Snowdon was having at Olympia. Snowdon, as ever, was charming and desperate to know what we thought of his pictures. They were very impressive. Ever since his marriage to Princess Margaret he'd had to live with the 'Ah well, he gets the work because of his title' syndrome, which I thought was unfair. His work had always been original and inventive, and as someone who's done a fair bit of photography, and knows only too well how difficult it really is, I think he's in the very top bracket. He was always a perfectionist. Way back in the late fifties he'd come to the Rediffusion Studios to take pictures while the *Show Called Fred* TV show was running, and I never forgave him for making me eat six custard tarts just to get an action picture right.

Pete was as impressed by Snowdon's pictures as I was, and on the face of it seemed the same as usual, laughing and joking, but the strain was starting to show itself. The tinted glasses were being worn a lot, and the bland, mask-like smile seemed to be getting more and more set.

He was, however, enthusiastic about his new film, which he was making with director Anthony Simmons. This was a story about a downtrodden busker, *The Optimists of Nine Elms*, and was being shot in real locations around London. As usual Peter had done a lot of research into the make-up, the voice, the clothes, to create a real, three-dimensional character. The pathetic little busker, wheeling his perambulator about the streets, with his performing dog sitting like a badly knitted hearth rug inside it, had a heart-breaking quality that owed a lot, I think, to Peter's present circumstances. It had the marvellous reality that he gave the early Clouseau, and the extraordinary Dr Pratt.

To extract that performance, at this time, from Peter hadn't been easy. Getting Everything Right Before The Teeth Went In was something Tony Simmons had to contend with. The teeth were artificial ones made especially by Stuart Freeborn, one of Peter's favourite make-up men, and were an idea Peter had for the part. Once all his make-up was adjusted Peter always became the character he was playing, so Tony had to make certain everything had been worked out before the false teeth were clipped on. The moment they were in place Peter became the old busker, and you couldn't really give direction to an aged, broken-down, music hall artist.

A highlight of the film was something which could have caused an even bigger problem, but Peter's own performance solved it. A major sequence saw the Old Busker, surrounded by hundreds of people at the start of a football match, trying to raise a few pence by busking. The scene was shot in the middle of a real crowd, at a real football match, and so perfect was his disguise that not one of those football fans ever realized that the scruffy old man, tottering about amongst them, was in reality Peter Sellers.

I sat alongside him at the preview of the film and, although I don't think the picture did very well financially, it was the best performance Peter had given for years. I hadn't seen him do anything as good since that wonderful unbroken run of acting performances in the late fifties and early sixties. And I told him so. He was delighted and thrilled at what I said, then told me in the next breath that it was all down to yoga, inner peace, meditation and a lot of good communication with the Other World. I knew perfectly well it was all down to Anthony Simmons having found the right combination for handling Peter and, more important, having the character to stand up to him.

If I ever felt there was a limit to Peter's unpredictability that thought vanished when a young lady called Liza came on the scene. In the middle of a new film with Roy and John Boulting, *Soft Beds and Hard Battles*, and still officially married to Miranda, Peter went to a concert in London given by Liza Minnelli, and had an attack of the instant attractions. The attraction proved to be mutual. At once they started the most public dalliance the British public had ever seen. Day after day the newspapers printed columns about Peter Sellers and Liza Minnelli, and they indulged the press in every way they could. No white spread fingers blanking out camera lenses, or buried heads in backs of cars. Holding hands publicly, they gave sugary interviews to the press, and quite open declarations of love were made. It was a three-ring circus. Once again Pete was up there with the great lovers, and only a faint whisper from odd quarters about the wisdom of talking of marriage when you already had a wife disturbed the romantic escapade. The studio where Peter was filming was under siege by the tabloids and, feeling unable to control either Peter or the press, the Boultings ceased production for two weeks, gambling the passion would cool. It did. Well, actually a clairvoyant settled the matter. To underline the farcical nature of the affair, Liza Minneli consulted one (Tarot cards a speciality), and he publicly predicted the marriage would not take place.

When I got the phone call it was obvious Pete was furious. 'Why didn't she ask my one?' he said. As it was obvious he was talking about his own pet fortune teller I declined to comment, but I was worried about the logic of his query. Unless you were a clairvoyant yourself who could foretell what his 'one' was going to foretell? As this train of thought was giving me a headache I didn't pursue it. All this happened during the two-week suspension of the film. The flame had burnt intensely, then died to a smoulder, and Pete went back to work. Sadly, the Boultings needn't have bothered. The film was, unfortunately, a flop.

Even more unfortunately *Ghost in the Noonday Sun*, Pete's next film, was an even bigger flop. A so-called zany comedy—and that description alone should have been a warning—it was filmed on location in Cyprus and concerned a group of pirates, one of them played by Spike Milligan, and their adventures on board their ship. The stories about the film became collectors' items. The pirate ship had a mast so tall it caused the boat to rock from side to side, making the craft totally uncontrollable; it couldn't even be steered into the sunlight they needed to film by. Then there were confrontations between Peter and Anthony Franciosa (his American co-star) which involved threats of bodily violence. The film's two producers finally left not only the production, but also the island of Cyprus. All in all a jolly happy affair. *Casino Royale* was by comparison a huge success. At least it got finished, and shown. *Noonday Sun* was never even completed.

The whole riotous disaster was catalogued in a long and involved calypso, written and composed by a member of the crew, which detailed, very comically, very musically, and very scandalously, the whole story of the fiasco. Libelling everyone concerned, the recording that was made of it could never be played publicly.

However, it did get a hearing. The last scene of the film that was actually shot had Peter and Spike buried up to their necks in sand, both quite helpless. As soon as the shot was over members of the crew, tipped off that this was to be the final scene, ran in, placed loudspeakers either side of Peter and Spike, and the calypso was played full blast all the way through. Unable to move, with just their heads above the sand, Pete and Spike were forced to listen to every line as the calypso told the history of the disaster. To Peter's credit he was the first to laugh.

* * *

The run of professional failures just had to end, and, thank God, Blake Edwards reappeared on the scene. The collaboration between Blake and Peter had already produced two of the funniest, and financially most successful, films of Peter's career, *The Pink Panther* and *A Shot in the Dark*, in both of which he'd played the accident-prone Clouseau.

Another Clouseau film had been made in 1968, but that one starred Alan Arkin. Peter had been offered the picture but, for reasons that were never made clear, he turned it down. It could have been money but I'm fairly certain it was to do with Peter not wanting to go on giving the same performance. *Inspector Clouseau*, as the Arkin film was called, didn't have any impact at the box office and it wasn't surprising. Alan Arkin gave a marvellous performance but the public wanted the tweed hat, the sad moustache, the white Private Detective From Every Hollywood Movie raincoat and, most of all, they wanted to see just what destruction Peter's Clouseau could wreak on the world.

Lord Grade, in London, arranged, and signed both Peter and Blake to make a television series, with Clouseau as the star, called *The Return of the Pink Panther*; as was quite normal practice, they would make a feature-length episode to start the series. To have to accept that the return of Clouseau was to be on television was, for Peter, a bitter pill to swallow. Films still held sway as the prestige medium and for a film star to make a television series, however opulent, was still considered to be going downmarket. It somehow signalled that this was to be the end to your name being in lights, and that now you were to be merely a part of domestic evening viewing round the fireside.

Cast by Blake to be the new *Panther*, I met him to talk about the character I was going to play. 'Well,' he said. 'What are we going to do with you this time?' Blake had very definite ideas about how he wanted me to look as I was going to play Pepe, a small-time crook haunting the back streets of Casablanca. 'A walking disaster zone,' Blake said. 'You've lived, eaten, and slept in your clothes for the last twenty years. I'll leave it up to you.' This was the grovelling part to end all grovelling parts, and with glee, plus the aid of the wardrobe mistress, I acquired a broken-down tropical suit, a tatty shirt, a string tie, and an old beaten-up straw hat. And then we were off on the road to Morocco, *Pink Panther* bound.

On 7 June 1974 we landed at Casablanca, and such is the power of the cinema that Pete and I kept looking for Rick's Café, and in the foyer of the skyscraper Marhaba Hotel, where we were staying, we kept expecting to hear a white piano playing 'As Time Goes By'. Casablanca, since the French had moved out, seemed to have gone to seed, but it still had that wonderful, North African smell. The air was dry and warm, and the first night of our arrival Pete and I had dinner, high on top of the hotel, with the Casablanca harbour lights blinking below. It would have been difficult not to love the glamour. To make things even better, Blake had brought along Julie Andrews, now his wife, plus their family.

Up in my hotel room I started working on my clothes for the film. The suit we'd got in London was perfect but not dishevelled enough. I had to get the look right. A Moroccan business man looked out of the window of his office one morning, three storeys up, and saw, right opposite him, a man on a hotel balcony rubbing an old suit on a concrete parapet for twenty minutes. Then he saw the same man run a flame from a cigarette lighter round the brim of a straw hat. Realizing by now that he was watching one of the Englishmen who, like mad dogs, had obviously spent too much time out in the midday sun, he didn't seem too surprised when, a few moments later, I reappeared on the balcony, wearing the now almost threadbare suit, and proceeded to pour half a bottle of Ambre Solaire all down the front of it.

The pièce de résistance were the canvas shoes the wardrobe mistress and I bought from the best shoe shop in the main street. We were assured they were of the highest quality but, twenty minutes later, they were in virtual ruin. Toes ripped open, laces replaced with dirty bits of broken string. We gave them some parapet treatment as well. Then we realized we were moving off to Marrakesh in a few days and we'd better get another pair as back-up. Keeping the shoes on to give them a bit of extra wear we walked back to the shop, where the sales girl, knowing I'd only had the shoes for twenty minutes, nearly had hysterics when I pointed to them and jokingly said, 'I thought you told me these were the highest quality.'

We all managed a dip in the hotel swimming pool most days, but the social life in Casablanca wasn't the most exciting thing we'd ever experienced. One night a small, badly typed, grubby notice appeared in the hotel lobby inviting the cast and crew to a party given by the Moroccan gentleman who supplied the film with all its transport. Well, no one got too excited. After all, as Peter and I agreed, why should a party given by the local transport manager be anything to get excited about? Which just goes to show how wrong you can be.

The night of the party there was a frantic phone call from our production manager. 'Graham,' he said, 'do me a favour and come to the party. No one's going from the cast, and only a few of the crew. Our Moroccan friend is going to lose a lot of face.' After that speech I could hardly say no, and one of a fleet of shiny black Cadillacs took us to what appeared to be a palace just outside the town.

The scene was incredible. Fairy lights were festooned everywhere, white-coated servants were in their dozens, and crates of every imaginable drink were stacked high. Whole sheep were being roasted on huge iron wheels. It was as if half a dozen of the richest men in the world had clubbed together to give a midnight picnic. I got to a phone fast and called Peter. 'Never mind why,' I said, 'all of you, get here now.' He got the picture and rounded up Blake, Julie, Christopher Plummer plus assorted actors. They clambered into the fleet of Cadillacs and were over in minutes. It turned out to be one of the greatest and most lavish parties I've ever been to in my life. God knows what sort of fiddle that transport manager must have been on, but who cared. Pete and I sat next to each other, cross-legged like opulent sheikhs, selecting delicious hunks of meat (only with the right hand of course) while watching fifty Berber dancers, who had been specially flown over the mountains to be the cabaret. Life on a film location can be hell, I tell you.

The next morning's filming was rather low key. An ashen-faced crew gingerly set up the lights while members of the cast, including myself, tried very very hard to concentrate on the lines we should soon be uttering. We were using the lobby of the Marhaba hotel for the scene where, as Pepe, I first meet Sir Charles Lytton, the eminent jewel thief, played by Christopher Plummer. He was great to work with, and it was during the scene we first set up the hilarious running gag of having my fingers broken. I had to munch salted peanuts throughout the scene, and the sound of every munch was magnified in my head a hundred times.

* * *

The flat plain, south of Casablanca, seemed an endless scrubland until, far in the distance, appeared a tiny, white-capped range of hills. As we got nearer they enlarged until they appeared for what they were, the Atlas mountains. After ten days of filming in Casablanca we were moving to Marrakesh, taking up residence at the Mamounia Hotel. Winston Churchill used to indulge in his hobby of painting there. The hotel gave Peter the Churchill suite, and from the balcony you could see why the part-time brick-layer, and full-time Prime Minister, came here to paint. The light was so clear you felt you could put your hand out and pat the snow on top of the mountains. Our lighting cameraman,

Geoff Unsworth, one of the best cinematographers in the world, and later an Oscar winner for his work on *Cabaret*, admitted he'd never seen anything to equal it. And I'd never seen anything to equal the Mamounia. This enormous hotel had been built in the late 1920s, when both money and space had been limitless. The dining room could have been a hangar for one of those giant airships of the thirties, and the bedrooms were spectacular. Every room had twin beds, both of which were king-sized. The balconies were immense, overlooking a swimming pool that made the Round Pond in Kensington look like a small puddle.

This paradise location, with Blake in charge, seemed to give Peter a big lift. It was great to see him back on form as Clouseau, if only for the selfish reason of standing behind camera and watching him get one of his famous attacks of the giggles. Peter, if anything, was worse in that direction and, during scenes he played with Dave Lodge, he had physically to hang onto the scenery he was in such a state. His then girlfriend Christina (Titti) Wachtmeister, tall, elegant, and very stylish, had come to join us in Marrakesh. This beautiful Swedish girl was in fact Countess Wachtmeister, daughter of the Swedish envoy to Washington. With the same delightful accent that Britt possessed, she did Peter's ego no harm as she lay by the pool side during the day, or danced with us at night in the hotel disco.

In my film clothes, my dishevelled appearance caused a sensation in the market-place of Marrakesh. I think it was the first time in history the natives felt like giving a European money. One morning, sitting with Titti on a balcony overlooking the main square, Peter invited me up for a drink. I hadn't been with them for more than a couple of seconds when a large Moroccan waiter appeared and tried his best to throw me off the balcony. He was convinced I was some sort of derelict trying to cadge free drinks. The running gag with my broken fingers meant that they were tied up every day with wooden splints. Finally allowed to have that drink, and unable to hold the glass, a large straw had to be provided. Pete couldn't resist working the old joke on Titti. 'You do realize, my dear,' he said, 'when my friend has to go to the gents he's going to find out just who his friends really are.'

Everything on the film was going beautifully until it came to Achmed the stunt man. In one of the big spectacular scenes of the film Christopher Plummer had to escape from an exotic Moorish palace where a giant party was in progress. A beautiful, scantily dressed belly dancer was rotating her stomach at an alarming rate in the foreground, while seated at a table just behind her was myself. The drums were throbbing, the extras were wolfing down the free food as if there was no tomorrow, and we all waited for the big stunt that was to be the climax of the scene.

Joe Dunne, the stunt double for Christopher, had to slide down a rope from a balcony right above my head and land on the table I was sitting at, crushing another finger. Normally stunts go right first time but something went wrong with this one. Joe Dunne, wearing an exact copy of Christopher's clothes, slid down the rope. The pulley jammed, for a brief moment Joe hung suspended, then fell twenty feet. Luckily, he broke his fall by landing on a pile of Moorish cushions but, by trying to hang onto the rope, his hands were so badly burnt he couldn't do the shot again.

That was when nemesis, in the person of Achmed, a Moroccan stunt man, appeared. He assured Blake, Christopher, Peter, and me that he, personally, was the best descender of ropes in the whole of North Africa, and please not to worry any more as Allah had ordained all would be well. Now, I wouldn't cast any reflections on the Muslim religion, but I can only suppose Achmed had been a bit of a naughty boy and Allah wasn't too mad about him at the time. All I can say is, that if the first stunt went slightly wrong, the second was a total disaster.

The drums throbbed again, the food vanished faster than ever, and Achmed grabbed the rope and launched himself into space. The rope jammed once more, and Achmed also fell twenty feet. He was large, well-built, very heavy, and was going at a fair rate when, missing the cushions, he hit me. He then bounced onto the marble floor, breaking both his ankles. The table was smashed and I lay among the wreckage convinced something terrible had happened to my lower half. Pete, who'd been watching the shot, was one of the first to pull me clear so I could be put on a stretcher. This was placed in the back of a dilapidated truck, which had a crude red cross daubed on the side. Off Achmed and I were driven at high speed through the winding back streets of Marrakesh, the driver clearing the way by steering with one hand, while shaking a large hand bell out of his window with the other.

At the hospital they got Achmed out and wheeled him away. Then it was my turn. The trolley I'd been put on had only been pushed a few feet when I suddenly made a miraculous recovery. I sat up explaining that all pain had vanished, and I would like a taxi back to the hotel. I gritted my teeth, managed to get into the cab, and was whisked back to the Mamounia, where the hotel doctor gave me a few painkillers to get me through the night. Back from filming, Peter came to my room, asking what was the secret of the magical visit-to-Lourdes type recovery. Quite simple, I told him. The secret was the sight of the blood stains that had never been wiped off the trolley that was taking me into the hospital.

The hotel pool was the centre of social life and apart from watching Peter stand on his head for at least half an hour at a time (he was very into yoga at this period), the other attraction was inspecting the various coloured bruises I had on my legs. Luckily nothing had been broken, but I gave an excellent impression of an exotic tropical fish while swimming in the pool. The ladies all looked adorable in their various bikinis (then all the rage), and everything was under control. That is, until on Saturday the Italian model arrived. About five-foot-five, with a beautiful figure, she smiled sweetly at everyone, lay on her sun bed, and took her bikini top off. Peter and I, like every other man round the pool, immediately got paralysis of the neck muscles and gazed fixedly at the sky, determined not to be caught looking. It was the women who were up on their elbows checking out this obviously appalling social behaviour. The next morning, Sunday, we all met again, everyone smiled sweetly and, without exception, every girl on the film unit took her top off.

Paradise had to come to an end, and *The Return of the Pink Panther* finished with our return to London, where we had a lavish end-of-picture party steaming down the Thames on a pleasure boat. Fairy lights were draped between the masts, the band played on the deck, and we all crossed our fingers for the film's success.

* * *

The marriage to Miranda came to an end later in the year, fortunately reasonably amicably, and Pete moved into a flat in a tower block in Victoria. I thought it was terrible, at least for him. It was if he'd deliberately chosen the most impersonal place in London to live. Large smoked glass doors led into a cathedral-sized lobby where a silent porter watched flickering monitors which were wired to security TV cameras dotted about the building. You crossed acres of fitted carpet to a lift which whooshed you silently to the third floor. More carpet to track across to a second lift, which silently took you up to the fourteenth floor. Watched by another security camera you crossed a tiny lobby, and went through a door into a flat that could have been anywhere in the world. Impersonal, soundless, and totally insulated. High in the air, at the top of this cornflake-box tower, Peter pottered with his gadgets, talked a lot on the telephone and was, if possible, lonelier than ever.

Pete was always partial to turning up at our

house on Sundays. To him this made sense as he was usually showing off a new car, and there'd be little traffic. However, one particular Sunday he arrived, wandered in forlornly and suggested we go for a drive. His conversation had all the hallmarks of nostalgia and sure enough his car, like a milk horse trained to make a well-worn round, almost steered itself. I knew just where we would be going.

Sure enough, just round the corner, a few hundred yards away, we passed the house where he, Anne, and the children, had spent seven relatively happy years. It boasted a miniature bijou cinema in the loft. Peter's sense of humour had made him put a sign over the entrance which read 'B.Jew'. Typical of Pete's obsession with detail, it even had a set of real, blue velvet cinema seats, bought when a local cinema was pulled down. Before selling the house to comedian Alfred Marks, Pete gave a farewell party, and during a firework display burnt most of the lounge to cinders.

Straight on to the main road, turn left and follow your nose to East Finchley. I joined in the nostalgia here as we were passing the flats where Pete had arranged for me to stay beneath him and savour the delights of the hot Dettol baths. Sharp right along Creighton Avenue and then left at Tetherdown. We paused outside the little house, the first that Peter had ever owned, still boasting the elegant, black wrought-iron railings he'd put there. For a little while Pete just sat in the car, nodding quietly. Then it was off down Muswell Hill Road towards Archway. I expected a detour to cut through to Highview flats, where he and Spike had been neighbours, but suddenly, abreast of Highgate Wood, Peter pulled up again. Puzzled, I gazed up at a three-storey block of flats. 'Southwood Hall,' I said. 'I lived there for three years.' Pete gave me a strange look. He pointed to a small cottage right next door to the flats. 'And I lived *there* for three years,' he said. I shook my head in disbelief at the extraordinary coincidence. Pete and I had lived next door to each other, as schoolboys, from 1936 to 1939, and never knew until that moment.

Poor Audrey, sitting in the back seat, now had to cope with two waves of nostalgia at the same time. I rambled on about playing in Highgate Woods, and walking up to Hampstead Heath, but Peter seemed very quiet. I looked at Audrey. 'You realize we were there as children, right next door to each other, and yet we never met until the end of the war, when we were airmen.' Then there was a strange noise. I turned and looked at Pete. His fingers were clutching the rim of the steering wheel, his forehead almost touching the centre of its spokes. His shoulders seemed to be heaving. 'Oh Christ,' he said. 'Whatever happened to LAC Sellers?'

CHAPTER FOURTEEN

TELL ME, DOES YOUR DOG BITE?

In November of 1974 there was a big RAF Gang Show spectacular at the Gaumont State, Kilburn, and in that mammoth theatre almost every surviving member of the wartime shows was in the audience. The television cameras were there (among others, Peter and I gave brief interviews), and there was a lot of jovial back-slapping. Everyone had reminiscences of the Burma Campaign, being in Italy at the siege of Cassino, playing to the Eighth Army at Alamein, landing in France after D-Day. Nostalgia was the order of the day. Considering how long ago we gentlemen had toured the world, playing in all those overseas camps, most of us looked reasonably well on it. The high spot of the evening came when a sea of fire glittered down through the aisles and Her Majesty The Queen, wearing a dazzling tiara, came and sat in the audience with us. At that reunion Pete and I realized we were also celebrating a thirty-year friendship.

* * *

The final print of *The Return of the Pink Panther* was finished, and, just like the old days, I got an excited call from Peter. He'd seen the completed film and was over the moon. 'It's going to be a beaut, Gra, and the broken fingers routine is marvellous, and wait till you hear the music Hank Mancini's put over your entrance.'

The first time I saw the picture Mancini was there, and it was fun to hear how he'd managed to insert a few bars of 'As Time Goes By' when dishevelled little Pepe walked across the hotel lobby. Even more important, after the screening, Mancini told me the powers that be had seen the film and had decided it was such a potential hit they were going to release it in the cinemas and forget all about it going on television.

Their judgement was proved right as *The Return of the Pink Panther* became one of the biggest grossing comedies ever known to the box office. All the old magic of Clouseau, plus the glamorous background of Morocco, worked miracles. Peter was a box-office champion once more and it was only a matter of time before another *Panther* would be scripted and directed by Blake. Peter kept up the unannounced appearances at the house (it was during this time we made our nostalgic trip to see Ted Ray) but the masochistic streak that kept him reminiscing about the past was still with him. Any photographs of the old days delighted him and every so often I caught him giving Audrey and me looks, as if trying to find out the formula for a happy marriage. Restlessness was his greatest problem. Looking forward to future work was fine, looking back at past happiness was fine too. He couldn't stand the present. A sure sign of his discontent was lack of attention. Nothing seemed to hold his interest for more than a brief time. Restlessly he jumped from novelty to novelty. He had always suffered from this but never as badly as now.

The one constant in his life was the flickering candle that burnt in the corner of the living room of the tower flat. This was a shrine, a permanent memorial to his mother Peg. To me it was understandable. What wasn't understandable was that now that yoga, standing on his head, and the general flirtation with Eastern religions was out, spiritualism was back in. Tarot cards, planchette boards, crystal balls, all the paraphernalia returned, and nothing you could do or say would shake Peter's belief in them. To be fair, he never tried to inflict any of it on me. Maybe because I'd made my feelings so obvious. Mind you, I always had a sneaking suspciion that had I burst in on one of the seances flourishing some new, exotic, video camera, he'd have had the lights switched on in a second anxious to try it out.

⋆ ⋆ ⋆

The 1970s was not only the age of Aquarius but of pot, reefers, and Cloud Nine, and it was purely a question of time before I got the invitation to join the club. Supposedly invited by Peter to the flat to admire a new camera, I found we were not alone. The ladies were both blonde, both wore mini-dresses, apparently knitted from thick, silver rope and both giggled a lot. Definitely not Peter's normal choice of lady.

With a great show of stealth he went to a large flower pot in the corner of the room, took hold of the stem of the plant that was in it, and raised it high, roots and all. From the bottom of the pot he then fished out a small, clear plastic envelope from which he produced some plump, badly rolled, cigarettes. These were duly passed round and lit. As I'd given up smoking early in the 1960s I tried to duck out but Pete was adamant. 'Don't be a spoilsport,' he said and demonstrated the smoking method. 'Right down into the lungs, hold it, then slowly out.' Well I took a drag, held the smoke in my lungs as instructed, nearly choked with coughing and then started to laugh. I don't think this was the effect Pete was after but I was helpless. Whatever plans he may have had for the evening went totally out of the window as I lay, weak and gasping on the settee. I never bothered with it again.

*   *   *

The Pink Panther Strikes Again struck again in Munich in April of 1976, and from the word go there was an added bonus. Sitting by my side on the plane to Bavaria was Lesley-Anne Down. Like most of the British male population, I'd fallen in love with her as she'd twirled across our televisions screens in *Upstairs, Downstairs*, and here she was, cast in the film as a provocative *femme fatale*, and proving to be just as delightful off-screen as on. We formed a friendship which I'm happy to say survives to this day. I dined at her house when I last worked in Los Angeles a couple of years ago and we spent most of the evening laughing about the hysterical days we spent on the *Panther*. And they were hysterical.

It started in Munich when Lesley-Anne and I found that the main film unit wouldn't be arriving for several days. Holding the fort was a small advance party consisting of Peter, producer Tony Adams, first assistant director Terry Marcel, and the accountant Kevin O'Driscoll. So there we were, just the six of us, killing time. Like the gentleman he always is, Tony Adams smiled a beaming smile at Kevin and said, 'I feel sure the film would wish us to cement future relations with the populace of Munich by eating amongst them.' He then told the hotel concierge the evening merited a table at Huppermeyers. The respectful bow he got back declared that Herr Adams was a man of taste, and taste was the operative word. In one of the most celebrated restaurants in Munich we had a meal that was a gastronomic heaven. And if we thought the food was good, the wine was unbelievable.

The aged sommelier, almost bent double by the heavy gold cup that hung by its chain round his neck, assured us that all the wines in the cellar were of the very best. 'Tonight,' Tony said, 'we want the best of the very best.' We all toasted the success of the future film, and as I took my first mouthful of wine I knew we were drinking nectar. Pete swallowed his and said, 'Oh my Gawd.' Tony gave a sheepish grin to Kevin and said, 'I couldn't resist it.'

In the cellars of Huppermeyers were five bottles of one of the rarest Grand Vin wines in Europe, and Tony had ordered all five of them. The sommelier handled each bottle like a baby and gradually they were emptied. The result was glorious to behold. Lesley-Anne's sublime face got even sublimer, Tony Adams's smile spread like the Cheshire Cat's, and Terry Marcel kept giving small groans of appreciation. Kevin's expression could only be described as seraphic, while Peter and I, seated beside each other, regaled the table with our own personal rendering of a heart-rending wartime ballad entitled 'A Group Of Young Airmen'. Sung with great feeling, it had been known to bring tears to the eyes of almost everyone who ever heard it, and we did notice that several of the elderly waiters were, in fact, shaking their heads as if in sorrow. I believe the bill for that dinner came to—and it was 1976—over £700 but, considering the film we were about to start making ended up grossing over a hundred and fifty million, it was money well spent.

The whole film unit, all eighty of us, was staying at a large hotel on the outskirts of the town and you needed a cab to get into Munich proper. Ten minutes after arrival the crew were grouped in the lobby, bemoaning that fact. This problem became suddenly unimportant as three large buses drew up outside the hotel. From these buses descended one hundred and eighty teenaged American girls, each waving a fistful of travellers' cheques, 'doing Europe' on Daddy's money. All thoughts of cabs into Munich vanished, and next day the indoor swimming pool was echoing to the shrieks and giggles of those one hundred and eighty young ladies while, sitting round the edge, were our crew, all suddenly converted to the belief that there was a God after all. To say that Blake had a happy crew for the rest of the picture was the understatement of the year.

I'd been commissioned by the *Sunday Telegraph* to shoot a set of pictures entitled 'My Favourite Leading Ladies'. In London I'd already photographed Mia Farrow, Joanna Lumley, Susan Hampshire, Diana Rigg and the lovely lady who'd co-starred in the last *Panther* film, Catherine Schell. Lesley-Anne was the perfect girl to complete the set and we had the chance to spend the whole day in the grounds and palace of Nymphenburger, and she was a wonderful model. Then Blake and the crew arrived and it was down to business.

On the film we were shooting at genuine locations which included the Bayerischof, one of the great hotels of Europe. This was to lead, by an extraordinary chain of events, to my playing with Peter one of the most famous scenes in the entire *Pink Panther* series.

It all started with Blake wanting me to play Adolf Hitler. Well actually he wanted me to play a hotel concierge, working at the Bayerischof, who happened to *look* like Adolf Hitler. It was the first, and only time, I ever argued with Blake in all the nine films I eventually made with him.

'Maybe I could look like General de Gaulle?' I suggested. 'I'm a bit short but I've got the nose for it.'

Blake was polite but firm. 'He's got to look like Hitler,' he said. 'That way we'll get a great reaction from Clouseau.' Never was a truer line spoken. 'But I tell you what,' Blake went on, 'we shoot it, and if it doesn't work we won't use it.'

I needn't have worried. There was something neither of us had reckoned with: the skill of Harry Frampton, the make-up man.

On the first floor, in a room given to us for make-up and wardrobe, Harry Frampton gave a final touch with a sable brush, stepped back and said, 'Oh, Christ.' Adolf Hitler was looking at him through a mirror.

'Now you see why I didn't want to play him,' I said. 'Even without the bloody moustache I look like him.' And it was true. The hair falling over the eye, the Chaplin moustache; the effect was terrifying. Even worse, the concierge uniform of dark trousers, plus double-breasted brown jacket with small gold crossed keys in the lapels, was almost an exact replica of the outfit Hitler often wore. Now came the real sensation. I had to walk down the main staircase into the foyer, where Peter, Blake, and the whole crew, were waiting. Even worse, members of the public were still using the hotel and were milling about the lobby. Peter took one look at me and got convulsions, Blake had hysterics, and several elderly Germans seemed to be getting a reflex stiffening of their right arms.

I could have told Blake there and then we were wasting our tme, but after all I had been made up, and the cameras and lights were all set, so we had to try and shoot. Totally and absolutely pointless. We started the scene by my turning to camera and in a high-pitched German voice asking Clouseau, 'Vot iss your pleasure?' Peter took one look at me and burst into laughter. Seventeen times we tried that scene, and seventeen times Peter collapsed. Sometimes as soon as I turned round, sometimes we did several lines. He started to imitate my voice, I started to imitate his. Maybe if we'd persevered we might have got through it, but then the old German lady came out of the lift. Obviously staying at the hotel she walked straight past the cameras and, seeing me standing behind the concierge desk, handed me her key. She turned away, stopped, turned round and peered into my face then, giving a slow, unbelieving, shake of her head, walked out of the front door. As the tears of laughter started to run down Peter's face Blake surrendered. 'You'd better go home,' he said to me. 'We'll think of something else.'

I flew back to London the next day, had a quiet week with the family, then got the message to fly back to Munich once more. Peter and Blake met me at the studio. 'I think we have come up with something even better,' said Blake, 'and I'm quite sure you will both manage to get through it this time.' The smile he gave us both was charming but with possibly just a touch of desperation in the eyes. 'We'll be shooting the sequence down at Hohenschwangau next week,' he went on.

Little did he know what was to come.

I read the scene, liked it (thank God not a hint of Hitler), and this time got the chance to suggest the wardrobe and make-up. 'Pinocchio's father,' I said. As I was playing an aged innkeeper everyone agreed the old woodcutter look would be fine, so, a few days later, the unit moved south.

As a child I fantasized about the magical creatures that must live in the Gibbs toothpaste castle. White and gleaming, high on a hill, its tall spires glinting in the sun, it typified every fairy tale. Two hours after leaving Munich our car rounded a bend, and there, in the far distance, perched high on the side of a mountain, was my fairy-tale castle. 'What,' I said, 'is that?' Peter gave a patient smile. 'That, my dear Gra, is where we are filming.'

Ludwig II, the so-called Mad King of Bavaria, didn't have a toothpaste advert to inspire him (which is probably why he lost most of his teeth even before his early death) but he had a bare mountain and the imagination to build one of the great fantasy castles of all time. When you stayed at Hohenschwangau, as we did, it was easy to understand the air of mystery, tinged with romance, that governed the young king's life. The layer of mist that clung to the surface of the Alpine lake, the great army of pine trees that marched up every slope of the magnificent mountains, the songs of the birds amplified by the natural acoustics of the surrounding peaks. One free afternoon Peter and I walked completely round the lake on the edge of which Ludwig lived as a child, and on that walk of some four or five miles we never met a single human being. Halfway round, we sat, like schoolboys, bathing our feet in a crystal-clear stream that ran down into the lake. Several of the famous swans who live on the lake, quickly glided in. There was a fair bit of wing stretching and some hissing going on. I don't know whether they thought our bare toes were some sort of new delicacy to nibble on but Pete and I got the message and moved on.

I watched the same swans through the window of the hotel room where, once again, I sat in the make-up chair of Harry Frampton, being transformed into my aged innkeeper. Harry did a magical piece of work and it was rather frightening to age to seventy-five in under an hour. The masterpiece was the beautiful wart he applied to the end of my nose.

Film making being what it is, the room we were going to shoot our scene in was probably the smallest in southern Bavaria. Just big enough to get in the camera, the crew that was necessary, Blake, Peter and myself. The sequence was one of those wonderfully logical bits of comedy, that was based on a very ancient, simple joke. Clouseau meets the old innkeeper, strokes a little dog and says, 'Does your dog bite?' The old innkeeper shakes his head. The dog then savages the hand of Clouseau who, outraged, says, 'I thought you said your dog does not bite?' The old innkeeper shrugs. 'That is not my dog!'

Well, it was quite different from the Bayerischof. Pete took some nice shots of me with my camera before the shooting so he knew what the make-up was like. We all managed to clamber into the set, then Blake made his fatal error. 'Got any ideas?' he said to me. Well, I had thought of a joke. As the old innkeeper, I was leaning over a dilapidated hotel desk, warning Inspector Clouseau of the dangers to be found up at the castle. 'How about if I puff clouds of smoke out of a large meerschaum pipe,' I suggested, 'and gradually Clouseau will disappear from view.' Blake grinned, Peter laughed, and the joke was in. Property men on films are amazing. Within seconds the biggest pipe I've ever seen, with a bowl the size of a jam jar, appeared.

'Take it easy on the tobacco,' I said. 'I gave up smoking years ago.'

They'd even thought of that. 'Don't worry,' they said, stuffing the bowl with what appeared to be about two ounces of desiccated seaweed. 'It's a herbal mixture. Couldn't hurt a fly.' Well, all I can say is it's lucky they hadn't put black shag in as I must have smoked about twenty pipefuls that day. Carried away with the joke, which certainly was getting a lot of laughs, I puffed away like the Flying Scotsman trying to break the record from London to Edinburgh, and Peter kept vanishing in a fog which would have done credit to Dartmoor on a November night.

By lunchtime my head felt as if it was stuffed from ear to ear with cotton wool, and as if the tympani player from the Royal Philharmonic was having a great time thumping both my temples. But the scene was going wonderfully. I was used to Peter getting the giggles, but this was worse than ever. Every time I blew a cloud of smoke over him he went into convulsions, and the hysteria spread. Blake started to join in, followed by the camera crew. I've never known a comedy scene get more laughs.

We broke for lunch and even laughed all through that. Finally, at about four o'clock, miracle of miracles, we somehow got it all done. The next day, with the rare achievement of having a hangover without taking a drink, I said goodbye to Pete, Blake and the crew, and flew back to London, ready to start a new film on the following Monday.

* * *

This was a different cup of tea altogether. I'd been cast to play the Court Jester to Charlton Heston's Henry VIII in *The Prince and the*

Pauper, shooting at Pinewood Studios. Wearing cap and bells, in a medieval court, there certainly wasn't any giggling going on, except perhaps at my comic appearance. Charlton Heston, Harry Andrews, and Rex Harrison moved majestically about the set with delicate madrigals coming from the minstrel gallery above. The informality of Blake changed to the formality of director Richard Fleischer. We stood in awkward groups, Fleischer called action, we spoke our lines, and that was that. After two days Rex Harrison—the Duke of Norfolk—who happened to be standing next to me, said, 'Has he actually spoken to you yet?' I had to tell him no. 'Thank God,' said Harrison. 'He hasn't spoken to me either. I thought it was something I'd said.'

On the third morning Charlton Heston decided it was about time Rex Harrison got beheaded. About to shoot this telling sequence, I saw a familiar face. Behind camera stood Blake Edwards with his arm affectionately round Richard Fleischer's shoulder. 'For Christ's sake . . .' he said, looking at me in my ludicrous cap and bells. 'Is there nothing you won't do for a laugh?'

At Pinewood, to shoot some special effects, Blake had wandered onto our set to say hello to his friend Dick Fleischer. He gave Fleischer a look, then pointed at me. 'What I want to know is, how come you're using a well-known drug addict like him?' To say he'd dropped a bombshell would have been an understatement. My mouth opened wide, Dick Fleischer gave a nervous smile, Charlton Heston suddenly started to adjust the garter round his leg while, with a concentrated air, Rex Harrison gazed into the middle distance. Blake saw the look of horror on my face and gave a grin. 'You mean you really didn't know what happened that day we filmed the dog scene?' I gave him a blank stare. 'We'll never know who,' he went on, 'but someone filled that pipe of yours with pot. Throughout that day you were as high as a kite. But I've got to hand it to you, you kept going.'

Suddenly it all became clear. The cotton wool in the head, the drum routine on the temples, the hysteria of the crew as that room filled up with smoke. Evidently, while Peter, Blake and I were having lunch, I was sitting at an angle of forty-five degrees, stoned out of my mind. 'How we ever got you and Peter to finish the scene I'll never know,' Blake said. 'The Hitler sequence in Munich was child's play in comparison.'

* * *

Once more, filming the *Panther* had been hilarious, and once more, as the preview of the film in December proved, the formula worked as well as ever. Beautiful scenery, lush production value, and the comedy as tried and trusted as ever. Peter may have rebelled against working to the straitjacket of Clouseau but the box office was king and, with whoops of joy, the public flocked once more to revel in the exploits of their favourite detective. The 'Does your dog bite?' scene became famous (the joke is still quoted today), and the fact that I was high on pot, and Peter was getting hysterics watching me, didn't harm it one bit.

CHAPTER FIFTEEN

ANYONE KNOW IF IT'S RAINING IN RIO?

To say actors are childlike is to pay them a compliment. When I think of children I think of imagination, generosity, and tantrums that are basically harmless. Couple that with the ability to entertain, and I don't think you've got a bad bunch but, just as children need parents, so actors would be lost without their agents. They are the barrier between us and managements who make dastardly attempts to pay us miserable pittances so we can appear on some stage or film set and make them millionaires. The ten per cent we pay our agent rewards him for settling the terms regarding billing, salary (note the order in which an actor puts priorities) and accommodation. He also deals with 'Does the artist get a car?' 'What about a stand-in?' and 'Surely just a few more lines in the second act wouldn't hurt.' All these matters are taken care of by our paterfamilias. In some cases, as with my agent Dennis Selinger, they are also obliged to play the part of best man, godfather to the children, and lifelong friend.

Dennis was also Peter's agent for some

twenty-five years and performed the same kind of functions for him. Dealt with the deals, checked out the scripts, became a close friend and, as often as not, stayed up half the night listening to his troubles. He also did a couple of things for Peter which weren't really covered by his ten per cent. He introduced him to two of his wives. The first one, Anne Hayes, and the last one, Lynne Frederick.

Dennis introduced Anne to Peter at a dinner party in 1951. He introduced Lynne to Peter at another dinner party, twenty-five years later, in 1976. Lynne was just twenty-one when Peter saw her and it was obviously a 'Some Enchanted Evening' moment for him, even though he had Titti Wachtmeister with him at the time. At 5 am the next morning, wilful as ever, he woke Dennis up with a phone call desperate to get Lynne's number. With the skill of many years of negotiation behind him, Dennis stalled long enough to pass a message to Lynne, giving her the option to call Pete. Later that day she did and the rest, as they say, was history.

* * *

The eagerly awaited gala première of *The Pink Panther Strikes Again*, at the end of 1976, made the front pages twice. The Odeon, Leicester Square, was the venue, and there were big headlines when it was announced that His Royal Highness the Prince of Wales would be attending. A few days later there were even bigger headlines when it was announced that Peter Sellers wouldn't. The tabloids had a field day. The customary line-up of the artists concerned with the film had been oganized, and the Royal walk down the line was all set to take place. The public had always adored the opportunity of seeing the courtly bow of their matinée idols, and watching the glamorous actresses vie with each other as to their depth of curtsy (the blaze of flash guns as each lady film star dipped low becoming brighter in ratio to the cleavage shown). However, Peter, running true to form, would have none of it. The Establishment that still enforced the rule that divorced personages were not welcome in the Royal Enclosure at Ascot felt the line-up at the première should not include Lynne, as she and Peter were not yet married. Furious, Peter assured all and sundry that, Prince Charles or no Prince Charles, he would boycott the première. Not only that, he'd never play Clouseau again. Well, that bit wasn't true, but he certainly didn't go to the première. Prince Charles duly walked down the line, shook hands with who was there, and then, showing a rather splendid sense of humour said, 'You know, I could have commanded him to be here tonight.'

* * *

Early in February of 1977 Pete came to our house and brought Lynne with him. All the latest dark-room equipment had to be demonstrated, the newest set of transparencies projected, there was the usual enquiry about the state of the vacuum cleaner and, last, but not least, Hospy had to be brought out and admired. This large, furry, purple toy elephant had been given to Christopher, my eldest son, when he was aged six, by Peter's mother Peg. Without fail, on cvcry visit, Pete took it in his arms, gave it a cuddle, ruffled its fur, then passed it back again. Finally, into the garage to inspect Dr Funk of Tahiti who was hibernating in a box of straw. The baby tortoise, so tiny when Pete christened him on the docks at Southampton, was now the size of a large soup plate which, considering how many of our plants he'd devoured over the years, was hardly surprising. We'd tried growing a few vegetables, well fenced off, but when we discovered Dr Funk had the climbing ability of Sherpa Tensing, we gave up.

Lynne gave every impression of being just as enthusiastic as Pete, and there was a sense of fun, reminiscent of the times we'd had with Anne, and I had the feeling Peter deliberately brought Lynne to the house as if he wanted the nod of approval.

We were trying out a new Polaroid camera in the lounge when my youngest son Timothy burst in on us. Seven years old, the original little blond page boy, he was adored by every woman that set eyes on him and Lynne was no exception. 'Ah,' she said and looked at me with her huge dark eyes. 'Now, if only Peter could give me a child like that I'd get pregnant tomorrow. The only trouble is . . .' her look now enveloped Peter as well, 'his children have turned out *so* badly.'

As I had known Michael, Sarah and Victoria from their childhood, and naturally held them in deep affection, this remark came as rather a shock. Also, on reflection, I was baffled by the logic. I always presumed the child a man has by one woman must be temperamentally different from one he has by another woman. However, one had to make allowances for youth, as Lynne was actually younger than one of the children she was talking about. The remark certainly didn't seem to bother Pete, as a week later, in Paris, he and Lynne were married.

In what must have been record time, Blake had *The Revenge of the Pink Panther* on the stocks, and Pete was the first to break the news that I would be playing Dr Auguste Balls, costumier extraordinaire, and brains behind the many disguises that Clouseau wore. I then read the script, and called Pete. 'Blake Edwards is a sadist,' I said. 'You realize I have to recite a poem to you about you having to have Balls. How are we going to get through that?'

Dr Auguste Balls, according to the script, was of mid-European extraction, very excitable, a crawler of repute, and obviously a con man of considerable quality. He was also an idiot. When working on any new character I shared a trick of the trade with Peter. Get the voice right first. This was an obvious hark-back to our radio days and, as imitation is the sincerest form of flattery, you invariably based it on someone you held in esteem. I'd always been a great fan of Akim Tamiroff. From his first appearance, back in the early thirties, in *The General Died at Dawn*, Tamiroff was the consummate character actor and could play anything from the sullen partisan in *For Whom the Bell Tolls* to outrageous comedy parts in dozens of Paramount pictures. The voice I chose was based on his.

After the usual discussion with Blake about make-up, we decided a small wig would be worn by Dr Balls, plus a moustache. In January of 1978 I went to Shepperton Studios to meet Harry Frampton, once more in charge of make-up, to have a wig fitting. Well, I didn't get to meet Harry, or fit the wig, but I did lunch with Blake, which altered the next four weeks of my life.

Arriving just before lunch, I looked for Harry

Frampton in the dining room but he wasn't around. Blake and Peter were. 'Why,' asked Blake, 'are you here?'

Direct questions require direct answers. 'I have come for a wig fitting,' I replied, 'as I shall be playing Dr Balls next Tuesday.'

Blake gave a polite smile. 'You may well be playing Dr Balls next Tuesday but we will not be here to watch you. We—' he indicated Peter and himself—'will be in Hong Kong.'

There was a slight pause, then I said, 'I see;' and lapsed into silence. Well, there really wasn't a lot more for me to say. Blake then explained they'd altered the schedule and were flying to Hong Kong earlier than expected as, for script purposes, they had to shoot there during the Chinese New Year. 'We're going to be away for maybe three or four weeks. We'll shoot Dr Balls when we get back.' Then he appeared to look halfway between Peter and me. 'Fancy going to Hong Kong?'

As Peter gave a nod and said, 'Great idea,' I naturally presumed the remark was made to him. But in fact Blake was talking to me. 'I don't know what we'll do with you but we'll think of something.' He then waved to Derek Kavanagh, the production manager. 'Graham's on the plane Monday.' And that was how I flew, with the rest of the unit, to Hong Kong for three and a half wonderful weeks.

Hung Hoy Fa Choy is the Chinese for Happy

New Year, and it seemed to be plastered on every building in Hong Kong. The plane came down at night time on the narrow strip that juts across the bay, and the sea of lights below us made it look as if every firefly in the world had decided to migrate, and settle in the same place. It was breathtaking. With thoughts of rejoining mainland China far ahead, Hong Kong had hit its height as the business centre of the East, and was bursting with energy and life. The hotels were fabulous. I was at the Excelsior and my room balcony not only overlooked one of the most spectacular bays in the world but, some fifteen storeys down, precisely below me, was the famous noonday gun immortalized by Noël Coward. Thump, it went, every day at twelve noon. Peter and Lynne were staying at the Peninsula Hotel, architecturally of the old colonial style, which boasted a fleet of black-and-white Rolls-Royces, permanently available for transporting their clientele.

Hong Kong had obviously been very carefully planned with Peter and myself in mind. Apparently the entire camera output of Japan for the past several years was piled high in half the shop windows of the city, the other half were full of watches. But we nearly didn't get to see anything.

The morning after our arrival we grouped in the foyer and gazed out through the windows at a rain storm that made a monsoon look like a dripping tap. Blake's eyes narrowed as he looked at the Chinese production manager. 'And how long does this go on?' Chinese etiquette demands that you do a lot of bowing, especially if you've got to impart bad news. The production manager's head started going up and down like a nodding dog on a rear car shelf. 'Must inform Honourable Mister Edwards you want Chinese New Year, you get rainy season. So sorry.' And he gave several more bows.

Blake then came out with one of the great lines (as far as I'm concerned) of the century. He looked slowly round at the crew and said, 'Anyone know if it's raining in Rio?' Without a pause someone said, 'I'll find out', and disappeared. For the next hour cables flew to and from Hollywood while the cast and crew sat around the foyer. We were advised to have our luggage ready as it was quite possible we might be flying on to Rio de Janeiro. Then, as suddenly as it had poured down, the deluge ceased, the sun shone, the crew stopped joking about the girls from Ipanema, and we were set to film in Hong Kong.

Pete and I were all ready to raid those camera shops. Within a few days we had our chance. We pressed endless camera releases, we inspected ranges of lenses we never even knew existed, and gradually became laden down with glossy brochure after glossy brochure. Pete was always a Leica enthusiast and in the Leitz showroom he was having a marvellous time trying out all their latest equipment. That was when I first noticed the trembling fingers.

Peter's illness, all those years ago, had receded so far back in time I never really thought of it any more. He always had a fetish about showing any signs of physical weakness, and if he ever was a bit off colour he assured you it was 'Just a touch of the lurgi.' The lurgi was a Goon Show word that covered all sorts of ailments, ranging from the dreaded Montezuma's Revenge, to creeping alopecia of the upper lip, and served as a comic assurance that there was really nothing to worry about. I'd have liked not to have worried about the trembling fingers, but I was suddenly overwhelmed with a terrible feeling of sadness. I quickly looked away, knowing that he was tryng to hide the shaking. We walked back to the hotel still gazing into almost every shop window. A dazzling display of electronic watches caught our eye, every face a mass of liquid crystal figures. I looked at Pete. 'Say what you like, there's nothing competes with roman numerals.' He gave a couple of his *Hmmns* and off we went.

Crossing the hotel lobby the next day, I heard a voice say, 'Packarg, Meester Starka.' I turned and saw a small, Filipino bell boy, aged about fourteen, his uniform pure white with silver buttons down the front, on his head a matching white pill-box hat bobbed as he handed me a gift-wrapped box. The formula was repeated. 'Packarg, Meester Starka.' He then turned, walked out of the hotel, climbed into a large black-and-white chauffeured Rolls-Royce, and was driven away. I opened the box, and there was the most exquisite roman numeral-faced watch I'd ever seen. Peter had especially sent the watch, the bell boy and the Rolls, just because I'd admired roman numerals.

As there was absolutely no way in which I could match Pete's generosity I at least made sure the suite that he and Lynne occupied at the Peninsula was full of flowers for the next few days. The Excelsior, where I was staying, didn't have a fleet of Rolls-Royces. Pete and Lynne had to settle for me, a taxi cab, and two florists. But they appreciated the gesture.

Every so often Blake would assure me he'd think of something for me to do to justify the trip, but in the meantime I spent a lot of time shopping with Bert Kwouk. Famous for playing Cato, the karate attacking manservant to Clouseau, Bert was a godsend in Hong Kong. He spoke Mandarin, the official language, fluently and what bargains I got in the shops there were all due to him.

Always a great one for novelty, and with his usual enthusiasm, Peter arranged an extraordinary meal one evening. In a private room of a Japanese restaurant, seated on three sides of a large hot-plate, were Lynne, Pete and me. Facing us, wearing a loin cloth, and wielding two large, fearsome-looking spatulas was a frenetic Japanese gentleman who went into a ballet routine that would have put Nureyev to shame. The sum total of his efforts was that we each got a three-inch square of steak, and forty-five minutes of juggling.

The filming went very smoothly but nobody expected to get through three weeks without at least one hysterical scene, and it came in one of the hotel lifts where Peter was well and truly hoist with his own petard.

Not many people know (even possibly Michael Caine) that petard means breaking wind. In the script, four gangsters, played by Robert Loggia, Tony Beckley and stunt man Dinny Powell, plus Peter in a fantastic get-up as a Michelin Tyre Man godfather, are standing in a lift. Somebody breaks wind; the comedy comes from each man being determined to show no sign of guilt. Behind camera a serious discussion took place as to who would make the noise for them to react to. Blake got the job. The camera turned over, the clapper board clapped and Blake, pursing his lips, blew what he obviously thought was an artistic fart. Well, it was pandemonium. Peter was in tears, Robert Loggia leant against the lift and shook with laughter, Dinny Powell shut his eyes and appeared to be praying, while Tony Beckley just quietly turned his face to the wall. They finally gave up, and put the noise in afterwards.

Incidentally, I never did get to film in Hong Kong, and I don't honestly think Blake ever intended me to. I suppose he reckoned it would be a nice trip for me. Well, he was right about that, and there was Auguste Balls to look forward to in London.

* * *

At Shepperton studios the designer of the film, Peter Mullins, had done Auguste Balls proud when it came to his shop. Weird costumes and wild disguises festooned every wall. Ancient dance tunes were played on an antiquated horn gramophone. As Auguste, I had to disguise Clouseau as Toulouse-Lautrec, and Peter's make-up was sensational. Kneeling down, with shoes jutting from his kneecaps, he looked only three-foot high and was getting laughs even before we started. As usual, the set was crowded. Both Lynne and Julie Andrews were there hoping for something extra to happen, and of course it did. I stole a line from *The Men*, which had starred Marlon Brando. Fervently I told Clouseau, 'You can walk, Inspector, you can walk!' Peter immediately did a piece of oneupmanship. He was just supposed to totter towards camera. Instead, totally unrehearsed, his tiny figure broke into song.

'Thank heavens for little girls, they keep on getting smaller every day!' Then, collecting a 'burm' with its fuse already burning, at the front door, he refrained from tipping the delivery man by explaining, 'I'm sorry, I'm a little short.'

By some miracle we didn't giggle once. However, we hadn't got to the poem sequence yet. A few days later we began to shoot that scene, and from the word go I knew it was going to be one of those days. There were comic traps and snares we would have to bypass to get to the safety of a proper take. My first appearance, for a start. Damaged by the 'burm' in the first sequence, I hobbled forward on a crutch, wearing a night-cap, a night-shirt, bandages wrapped round my head like a mummy, plus a large piece of sticky plaster across my nose.

Dyan Cannon, a very glamorous Hollywood film star, and once wife of Cary Grant, was in the scene with us. Very professional, but not possessing a particularly eccentric sense of humour, she was totally baffled as she saw Peter fighting not to laugh. He got past that trap all right, but when it came to grasping my heavily bandaged hand, which made Auguste give a desperate cry of pain, he didn't stand a chance of avoiding the snare, and started to laugh. Baffled, Dyan Cannon looked at Blake. Blake grinned and said, 'You've seen nothing yet.'

And she hadn't. Once past the handshake I had to blow into a speaking-tube, which immediately spurted clouds of dust into my face. We had to do that bit at least six times. Finally, the real pitfall of the scene where Auguste assures Clouseau, poetically, of his allegiance. I dramatically struck a pose, tried hard not to catch Peter's eye and launched into my stanza.

Through wind and mud, snow and hail,
Whether long or short, dark or pale,
Remember that, when duty calls,
You've got Balls!'

Well, we tried; God knows, we tried. Eight times we tried. At last Peter sat in his chair at the side of the set, dabbing his eyes with a paper tissue. 'Sorry, Blake,' he said. 'It's no good. I know I'm supposed to look at Gra, but I can't. I just can't.' Luckily, there was a solution. On one take I'd got halfway through the poem before Peter collapsed. While he retired to the comparative sanity of his dressing room they took a close-up of me reciting the rest of the poem gazing at the empty space where Peter had been standing.

For me personally it had been one of the loveliest *Panthers* to make. The trip to Hong Kong, the fun shooting Auguste Balls, and the general enjoyment being around Peter when he was under the discipline of Blake. I mightn't have been so happy if I'd known it was to be the last *Panther* we'd ever make together.

CHAPTER SIXTEEN

THE PRISONER OF VIENNA

Having finished the filming of the *Panther*, my life suddenly became a frantic mixture of studying colour negatives on light boxes, of viewing transparencies with a projector, and checking the density and contrast of a few dozen black-and-white negatives. Kodak had decided to hold an exhibition of my photography. It was a magic time. To see one of my 35mm transparencies blown up to a colour enlargement four-foot square was a sight indeed. Luckily there were enough good pictures to make the exhibition very successful. It was held in the middle of April 1978 but unfortunately Pete was in America. He missed seeing a wonderful blow-up that had been made of a photograph I took of him on *The Magic Christian*, which, in many ways, portrayed him very much as I knew him. Not just the manic Goon Show comic, or the accident-prone Clouseau funny man, but a rather sad, wistful person, always trying to go backward in time.

He wasn't so wistful when he called from America a couple of weeks later. The way he described the new film he was about to make was very funny. 'It's *The Prisoner of Zenda*, we're going to make it in Vienna, got a marvellous part for you, you'll be acting with a large Saint Bernard, we'll have a great time.'

Sadly, we didn't have a great time, and the reason gradually became clear. Peter had agreed to do the film for Walter Mirisch, one of Hollywood's most august producers, but within a short time disagreement had set in and Peter tried to back out. However, money advances had been paid, contracts seemed to be watertight, and against his wishes Pete had to make the film. Not the best way to start.

On the surface all seemed reasonably well until I met director Richard Quine. He'd made some good films, and was an old friend of Blake's, but didn't have the same forceful personality. A delightful man, he seemed from the start to have to tread carefully. For obvious reasons, the script of a film has to be finalized before any shooting begins. Expensive costumes have to be made, expensive sets have to be built. Quine was a bit evasive. We may do this, but we may not do that, and perhaps we'll get the chance to to something else.

Then all was revealed. Peter called me again, clearly unhappy with the script and, out of the blue, asked if I'd do some work on it. Peter was playing the twin roles of King and Commoner and he'd opted to make the Commoner very common indeed. The Englishman who helps to save the throne of Zenda was to be a London cabby, and one of the scenes I wrote was to be a love scene for him and Princess Flavia in cockney rhyming slang. Given the chance, Pete would have made it very funny but, as relations became more strained, script changes suddenly became very low on the agenda. It was on that rather sombre note that in mid-July 1978 we went to Vienna.

I was as mad about Vienna as I had been about Munich. Always a sucker for towers, turrets, and castles, I loved to walk through the old sections of the city, marvelling at the sheer expertise of those early builders. I sat in Demels and munched unbelievable cream cakes, imagining the waltz kings were still playing their music in the nearby gardens, and the Royal Palace, where most of the location work took place, I could never get enough of.

The first sequence we shot in the botanical gardens had Peter and the rest of us, all dressed in our Ruritanian finery, playing a game of croquet, and it looked as if time had stood still. Elke Sommer, whom Pete and I had last worked with on *Shot in the Dark*, was in the cast, as were Lionel Jeffries and Jeremy Kemp. Lynne was playing Princess Flavia and was looking very ravishing in her period dresses. Always having my camera with me, I managed to get plenty of pictures.

The setting, and the clothes made it all look sumptuous, but at the heart of every successful film is the script. Although it wasn't down to the level of *Casino Royale*, with flimsy bits of paper wafting about, it was plain that Peter was making a lot of changes, and it was a case of the director trying to referee between the star of the film and the producer, and you never get much thanks for being the middleman.

Dressed in my livery, as Eric, chief dog minder to the House of Zenda (the St Bernard never stopped upstaging me), I sat in the make-up room looking at my face at seven o'clock in the morning. Not the best time to view yourself. I gave a sad shake of my head as I viewed my reflection. Lynne, sitting in the next chair, gave a laugh. 'Why don't you have a nip and a tuck like Pete's just done?' she said. I found out later he'd had some minor cosmetic surgery in America. That was the first time I'd heard of it.

As I had a short break from shooting I flew back to London the next day, and saw a photograph of Peter published in one of the morning papers. It showed him on location, in costume, on the film and was a candid picture, probably taken with a long lens. Mid-morning he called me from Vienna. We chatted about this and that, then, over-casually, he asked if the picture in the paper was mine. 'I've never sold a picture of you,' I said, 'and I don't intend to start now.' He apologized and rang off. That same day the publicity man on the film was summarily fired for allowing that photograph to be printed—because it showed Peter had a double chin.

Those trembling hands in Hong Kong had given a hint of Pete's health, and now things began to accelerate. The major symptom was his sheer irascibility. Obviously unsure about the script, disliking the producer, and being a dictator to the director, Peter's fuse was getting shorter and shorter.

Yet he could be just as funny, delightful and extravagant as ever. In a small drawer in my desk is one of my most valued bits of memorabilia. A miniature booklet with the legend on the front HOTEL BRISTOL, VIENNA. It opens to announce on its first page: 'Happy Birthday Lynne, Vienna, 25th July, 1978.' Beautifully engraved, the booklet opens further to tell you that the dinner about to be served will start with Beluga Mallossol Caviare, followed by Vichyssoise. A main course of Châteaubriand with Sauce Béarnaise, followed by Fresh Strawberries. The wines were Dom Perignon 1970, with a Nuits St Georges 1969. A copy of this small booklet was given to each guest.

In a beautiful candlelit room there were just twelve of us round the table. I was seated next to Pete who looked at me and said, 'I think we'd better have some music.' With that he went to the door and ushered in a small, elderly gentleman, carrying what looked like a typewriter with legs. The legs were extended, the top opened, a stool provided, and composer Anton Karas started to play on the zither his *The Third Man* theme: one of the most famous pieces of film music ever written, inextricably linked with the city of Vienna. It was typical of Pete to get him there that night just to play us through the meal: if the Strausses had been alive he'd probably have got them there as well.

As Vienna has always been the home of pastries, the birthday cake was beyond belief. Lynne puffed her cheeks and with one, long, curving blow every candle flame vanished leaving a circle of smoking wicks. On my other side sat Walter Mirisch's wife Pat, who was sheer delight and, as we reduced the levels in all those vintage bottles, inevitably Peter and I sang our heart-rending ballad, 'A Group Of Young Airmen'. It only needed a small amount of alcoholic beverage to unite Peter and me in our desire to bring this item of culture to the great restaurants of Europe. We didn't ask Anton Karas to accompany us as we felt some of the harmonies might be a bit difficult for him but we noted that he too, like the waiters of Huppermeyers, shook his head, we presumed with emotion, as we finished. We modestly took our applause, and to end the evening signed each other's menus, and I can look at them even now. Lionel Jeffries wrote 'You're a one-off,

Graham'. Next to that Richard Quine wrote 'You're a two-off!' Not an evening to forget.

I came down to earth the very next night. Jeremy Kemp (playing the villain Black Michael) had arrived and we dined together in our hotel restaurant. Across the crowded room Jeremy spotted a young, pretty girl, whispering to a friend and looking in our direction. Jeremy gave me a knowing look and in his wonderful rich voice said, 'Recognition, I believe.' With that the pretty girl started across the room towards us. 'One of us,' said Jeremy, 'is going to be lucky.' When she was a few yards away it became clear the girl was looking at me. 'And it's obviously going to be you,' he added. I put on the 'One just has to expect to be recognized in public' face while she stood at the table, gave a delicious smile and said, 'I believe you're Timothy Stark's father.'

Jeremy gave a snort and pretended something had gone down the wrong way while I did my best to put a brave face on it. The young lady had, in fact, worked with my little boy who, at the age of eight, was already a child actor. She was in Vienna looking for locations for a television film and had spotted me.

The war on the movie continued. Anything that Walter Mirisch liked Peter felt obliged to dislike, and the film suffered badly. By this time the atmosphere made all logical decisions impossible. While director Dick Quine was trying to shoot a scene, two opposing factions were giving him totally opposite instructions. Mirisch wanted a close-up, Peter suggested a long shot. As a consequence the film schedule went to pot and it overran its budget. Finally, I came back to London and Pete went off to Los Angeles to finish off the trick double shots before the final edit. But the editing didn't help. Though a beautiful-looking, and very expensive movie, it was sadly a stinker. One of the few joyous moments was a wonderfully comic performance by my old friend Norman Rossington playing a jailer in love with both his job and his instruments of torture.

Considering the state of his health it was amazing how much physical action Peter went through in that film. There was no indication of frailty, maybe it was because at last he seemed to have stopped his mania for slimming. But I'd always been amazed at Peter's sheer physical strength. Way back in our dining-in-Paris days, with Anne and Audrey, there'd been an occasion when the rich food took its revenge (we later found it was an allergy to coffee) and I staggered to the toilet white of face and moist of brow. Bent double, and retching, I was joined by Pete. Without further ado he grabbed me round the waist, tucked me under his arm and effortlessly half-lifted me off the ground. He then poured what seemed like half a bottle of Fernet-Branca down my throat. Undoubtedy one of the foulest-tasting drinks of all time, it nevertheless did the trick.

* * *

At the beginning of 1979, by a strange coincidence, we were both filming in America. I was gambolling on the beaches of Miami, filming *There Goes the Bride* with a young, pretty girl called Leslie Hornsby, better known as Twiggy, while Peter was in North Carolina, at the Vanderbilt mansion, making what was to be one of the greatest successes of his career, *Being There*.

Back in England, at Pinewood Studios, we'd finished off the *Bride* film then, suddenly, it was found the picture was undertime. A new sequence, featuring Twiggy and myself, plus an American psychiatrist, was hastily written and, at two days' notice, I flew to Hollywood for the very first time. The huge, legendary, nine white letters, spread over the hillside, almost overlooked the grounds of the mansion we were shooting in. Twiggy was already there and introduced me to the American actor who was to play the psychiatrist. The sun glinted on the bald head, the thick horn-rimmed glasses swivelled in my direction, and the big, white teeth glistened in a smile as Sergeant Ernie Bilko gave me a bear hug. 'Love your work sweety, just love your work!' It was Phil Silvers in full action. He was magic.

There was nothing wrong with the length of *Being There*. It was a perfect jewel of a movie and, glinting in the middle, was the extraordinary performance that Peter gave as Chance, the gardener. Simple, moving, tasteful, it highlighted Peter's ability to go that much further into a character, and helped to blot out much of the mediocre work he'd been doing in the recent past. Chance was up there along with Kite and Quilty, The President and Dr Strangelove, Dr Pratt and the early Clouseau. From head to foot it was, in every way, a completely masterly performance. The plodding walk, the sweet contented smile, the childish delight, the comic bewilderment, it was an astonishing *tour de force*. The performance also had something that hadn't been around for many years, Peter's personal approval.

For once, with *Being There*, he seemed very happy with the way a film had worked out. In fact he couldn't hide his feelings about it. Coupled with the natural, understandable, superstitious fear of counting your chickens before they hatch, he really did think he had a good performance on screen. But Pete was still as much as ever in awe of those pre-war film stars. He was thrilled to have worked on *Being There* with Melvyn Douglas. Once one of the most debonair of Hollywood's leading men, he was now an Oscar-winning character actor. 'Do you know,' Pete's voice was reverent. 'He played opposite Greta Garbo three times!'

CHAPTER SEVENTEEN

BIT OF A YO-YO, WHAT?

The roller-coaster of Peter's private life continued in its own apparently uncontrollable way. As he'd proved with the Liza Minnelli episode, he seemed quite unabashed at revealing publicly his most private life. In a bizarre interview with journalist David Lewin, in London in mid-1979, which naturally made the front pages, he spoke of yet another marriage being over, which apparently Lynne, still in America, knew nothing about. However, after some acrimony, this breach seemed to be healed and on his next film *The Fiendish Plot of Dr Fu Manchu* she was appointed a production executive.

Prior, and parallel, to this, was the disappearance from Peter's immediate circle of some of the people who had been closest to him in the past. Dennis O'Brien, his business manager, was one of the first to go, as well as John Humphries, his lawyer for many years (he'd been the brains behind the arrangement when Dave Lodge and I had owned Peter). The most extraordinary parting was with Bert Mortimer. One could never imagine seeing Peter without Bert being around somewhere, and he never found out why he was asked to leave. His departure, coupled with the break-up with the others, left Peter more and more isolated.

There were a few of the usual phone calls but the strain was beginning to show. There was a dejection in his voice I'd never noticed before, but he kept up constant reassurances about feeling fine. All set to spend some time in India I wished him lots of luck on *Fu Manchu* and packed my bags for the glamorous beaches of Goa.

The tiny enclave of Goa, on the mainland of India, was the setting for the film *The Sea Wolves*, which was shooting from November 1979 to February of 1980. Gregory Peck, Roger Moore, David Niven and Trevor Howard headed the cast of this action movie, based on a true World War II story. We did a lot of night shooting in the huge harbour of Goa on board a big, old freighter. All through the night, little motor boats would chug across the moonlit water ferrying actors and technicians to and from the shore.

At 3 am one morning David Niven and I were dismissed from the night shoot and were the only occupants, apart from the Indian helmsman, of one of the little boats. The trip took about twenty minutes. Above us was the spectacular sky of the southern hemisphere. Rows of glittering stars laid out like diamond necklaces on black velvet. We sat and marvelled for a while, then suddenly David, without any prompting from me, started talking about Peter in his wonderful pre-war public school manner. 'Bit odd, your chum Sellers, don't you think? I mean the way he goes on. Changeable and all that sort of thing. Never quite know where you are with him. Bit of a yo-yo, what? Up and down. All the time, up and down. Still, lovely feller.' The short sentences, dry and decisive, gave a summing up of Peter I never heard equalled.

Next day on the beach I watched David come out of the sea and flop, face down, on the sand about ten feet in front of where I was sitting under a palm tree, reading. Unaware of my presence he propped himself up on his elbows and, cupping his fingers together, started to try to pull them apart with all his might. He strained and strained. I thought at first it must be some isometric exercise but it was more desperate than that. Only after he'd pulled for several minutes did he finally flop on his back to sunbathe. Later, much much later, I realized I had been watching the start of his desperate fight to ward off the dreadful muscular disease that finally killed him.

⋆ ⋆ ⋆

I was back in England by the middle of February 1980 and about to start working on a sword and sorcerer picture *Hawk the Slayer*, directed by Terry Marcel. There were rumours about *Fu Manchu* which Peter had completed in Paris just before Christmas. Once again it had not been, I gathered, a happy film nor, as it turned out later, a very successful one. But Pete was thrilled with the news about *Being There*, which had been a big hit in the America. The critics were eulogizing once more and the words 'Oscar-winning performance' were being bandied about. It was obvious his career was climbing back up again. He went off to Ireland to make some television commercials, and then I got one of his calls. 'It's Dr Balls again for you,' he said, thereby informing me I would be once more playing Auguste Balls in the new *Panther*.

Peter and Blake had finally decided to part company and Peter, plus co-writer Jim Moloney, were scripting *The Romance of the Pink Panther*. Never the one to worry about the cost of a phone call (he was in Switzerland at the time), Pete read out great sections of the script and it did sound hilarious. It seemed that, as Balls, I was to disguise Clouseau at one stage as an armchair! We even had a bit of the dialogue in that famous accent over the phone. Or should I say 'phern'.

* * *

As expected Peter was nominated for an Academy Award for his performance in *Being There*, and on television the annual spectacle of the nominees, each in their own small individual square trying hard to look non-committal, made it more of a gladiator sport than ever. Peter wasn't present (his square was occupied by a still from the film). The envelope was ripped open, the card pulled out, and Dustin Hoffman was the winner.

There was another chance for Peter to gain official recognition for his performance in *Being There*, this time at the Cannes Film Festival, but once again another actor's name was announced. Michel Piccoli took the 'Best Acting' Award. Dennis Selinger had lunch with Peter at Cap d'Antibes the next day and he saw how deeply hurt Peter was at this second rejection. And I saw the television interview Peter gave at the Festival, which was screened in England, it came as a dreadful shock. There sat a small, white-haired old man, doing his very best to be wry and humorous, and I found I could hardly look at the screen. Although we'd talked on the phone a lot, the last time I'd actually seen him was just before the trip to Goa. Peter had looked like this before, but only after he'd spent an hour in the make-up chair being worked on by Harry Frampton. He was shrunken, stooped, and that marvellously clear voice had a frail, gasping note to it.

The cameras cut to another piece of action and I switched off the set. As the picture shuddered to a small white dot in the centre of the screen the telephone rang and a voice said, 'Have you just watched your friend on television?' The voice belonged to an eminent doctor I had known for many years, both as a physician and as a close friend. Someone I had so much faith in I had recommended him to Peter who, in his turn, had been treated by him. For a while all was well until one day Pete, working on a film, demanded that the doctor come to the studio and give him treatment. It was explained that all the necessary equipment was at the clinic and Peter had to come to Harley Street. That, as far as Pete was concerned, was the end of their relationship. On the phone I heard the doctor saying, 'What a tragedy. I regret to say he'll probably be dead in six months.' Well, he was being charitable. It was two months.

Peter's last trip to London, from Switzerland, on 21 July, was for the purpose of a reunion Goon Show dinner with Spike Milligan and Harry Secombe. He took up residence in the Dorchester, always his favourite hotel, and it was there he had the final heart attack which led to his admission to the Middlesex Hospital. For some thirty-six hours, that extraordinary physical strength, aided by a life-support machine, kept him alive. But finally, at 12.28 am, on the morning of Thursday the 24 July 1980 he died. He was fifty-four years of age.

* * *

A miniature monsoon hit London the day of the funeral. It was a sort of blessing as it somehow kept the affair at a low key. Not too many spectators, although a bevy of cameramen, getting drenched to the skin, hovered round the entrance. The small waiting room at the side of the chapel had the faint mustiness such rooms always seem to have; it mingled with the smell from the damp clothes of about thirty mourners who were crowded in there. Even umbrellas hadn't saved us from the rainstorm, which had now got to the level of a Hollywood horror film. Rumbling thunder, and great flashes of lightning, made it seem even more theatrical.

Slight nods of the head to each other, and occasional handshakes, were as far as the social niceties went. Naturally, Harry and Spike, of the legendary Goon trio, were there and of course Dennis Selinger. Tony Snowdon and I exchanged glances, and he gave a sad, wry shrug. Dear 'lightly oiled' Dave Lodge nodded, as did film critic Alexander Walker. Michael Bentine, as ever sporting his Old Etonian tie, stood near Evelyn de Rothschild, while Theo Cowan, publicity manager to Peter for as long as I can remember, and a good friend to us all, tried as much as he could to control the mounting press fever outside.

Canon John Hester was to conduct the service. It was right and fitting that he should officiate on this day of all days as he had been a close friend, and counsellor, to Peter for many years. We dutifully filed in to the small chapel, where a few moments later we were joined by Britt, who slid in at the back, to sit next to Spike. As Victoria, Peter's daughter by Britt, was naturally to be present, and as she was only fifteen, Britt had asked Peter's son Michael if she could come to the service to make sure her daughter was all right. As Britt had always shown great kindness to Michael and Sarah he gave her permission. The public appetite had been whetted with vague hints about Britt's appearance upstaging Lynne's official position as widow, but nobody need have worried. She mouthed a silent hello to Audrey and me, sat quietly through the service, disappearing at the end.

Then Lynne came in. She hung onto Michael's arm for support, sobbing profusely. John Hester gave a short, moving address and then suddenly Peter's final marvellous gesture was on us. He'd always stated that Glenn Miller's recording of 'In The Mood' should be played at his funeral . . . and it was. The hymns that had been played had been soothing, and

John Hester's words were quiet and comforting, but I have to admit that, up to then, I hadn't felt a lot of emotion. However, as the famous doo-doo-doo-doo-do of the saxophones blared out in the chapel followed by the dah-dah of the trumpets I found it hard to swallow. There, in my mind, clear as day, was Leading Aircraftman Peter Sellers, smart as paint in his best Air Force uniform, confidently gliding across the dance floor at the Nuffield Centre, holding a pretty WAAF in his arms. I suddenly had the absurd idea that if I looked up I'd see the obligatory spotlit crystal ball rotating above our heads.

Back at the Dorchester, where Lynne had moved up to the Harlequin suite, we went through the awkward post-funeral socializing. Lynne started to sob again. She cried out, 'He was too young to die!' Standing by me, near the french window (the suite boasted a terraced balcony), Michael, his face flushed with sorrow, looked at me. 'Lynne's having a bad time, but she's being very brave. She's super.' He couldn't have been more solicitous. Victoria, who I had once photographed as a small, divine-looking little girl aged four, now stood, a tall young girl, her head leaning on a door frame. She was deathly white, her eyes red from weeping, while Sarah, Michael's sister, sat in the middle of a settee, with the look of unbelief that the death of someone close brings. From their earliest years I'd seen each of these children gambolling about in the grounds of the various houses Peter had owned. It was a sad time. Finally, slowly, we drifted away, each of us mumbling the conventional clichés of sympathy.

* * *

Peter had always been able to command a lot of press coverage. After his death it was just the same. The details of his will were published and the news that Lynne was the main beneficiary and that Michael, Sarah and Victoria had been left only token sums—thus making it, the papers assured us, impossible for them to challenge the will—guaranteed the front page.

His closest friends—Dennis Selinger, Dave Lodge, Max Geldray, Spike, myself and others—found this news difficult to comprehend. We all of us knew of his legendary generosity and to find that not only had his children been eliminated from his will, but in such a way as to prohibit them taking any action about it, seemed to us to be almost beyond belief.

Spike Milligan had talked to Peter on the telephone a few days before his final trip to London. After finalizing arrangements for the reunion Goon Show dinner in London, Peter suddenly admitted he'd cut his children from his will. 'But I've been a bloody fool,' he said. 'I'm going to fix that when I come to London.' Tragically he died too soon. The terrible publicity about the will, which reflected badly on Pete, made Spike write to Lynne telling her of his telephone conversation. As he had read that Lynne was making the point that she was merely carrying out Pete's wishes, Spike felt he ought to inform her what Pete's last wishes were. The reply was a brief but adamant letter. The will stayed as it was. Lynne's letter hangs today in a glass-fronted frame in Spike Milligan's lavatory. Alongside it is a note which reads: 'In case of dysentery, please break glass.'

A few days later the head of public relations at Kodak, Derek Liley, approached me and said Kodak would like to mount a posthumous exhibition of some of the very fine photographs Peter had taken over the years as a tribute to him. Could I contact Lynne for them? As they'd done such wonders with my pictures I felt sure that Lynne would be pleased on Peter's behalf. I got through to the Dorchester and spoke to her. 'Kodak are suggesting a posthumous exhibition of Peter's photographs as a tribute to him,' I said. 'I know he would have been very flattered.'

Lynne's reply was immediate. 'Ah well, you see, I was thinking of bringing out a book of Peter's photographs myself, and an exhibition like that might jump the gun, mightn't it?'

I broke this news to Kodak. Some six months later a lady from a publishing house telephoned and asked if I had any photographs taken by Peter and, if so, could they have them to publish in a book, with a foreword by Lynne? I said I'd call them back, but I'm afraid I didn't.

* * *

The memorial service was held on 8 September 1980 at St Martin-in-the-Fields in Trafalgar Square. By bitter irony, had he lived, it would have been Peter's fifty-fifth birthday. Dave Lodge and I were two of the ushers. In contrast to the dreadful storm that had raged during the funeral it was a lovely day. Photographers and TV crews, plus a large crowd of spectators, spread across the steps that led up to the church, which always had such strong connections with the theatre, while inside we, the ushers, did our ushering. It was a fair turn-out. There were some surprising absentees, but by and large a lot of genuine friends turned up. Michael Bentine in full morning dress, was the representative of the Prince of Wales. Lord Snowdon read the Twenty-third Psalm, and Harry Secombe filled the church with his rendering of 'Bread of Heaven'. Finally, the slim, elegant, David Niven climbed up into the pulpit and gave, as one would expect, an elegant address, telling of the time he and Peter had discussed memorial services. 'No one will come to mine,' Pete had said. Niven gave one of his most delightful grins, looked down at us and said, 'Well, all you chums are here.' He never mentioned a yo-yo once. When the service was over I walked back through the morning sunlight to where I'd parked my car, climbed in, and drove home. The era was ended.

* * *

It's just ten years since Peter died but, fortunately, in the corner of most homes, is the rectangular screen on which his movies are repeated again and again, particularly the *Pink Panthers*. The laughs they get have outlived any of the scandal. Even more important, to me at any rate, is the video I possess entitled *The Gift of Laughter*. This was a Hollywood tribute to the bicentennial celebrations of Los Angeles, and is a compilation put together by the Motion Picture Academy of all the great comedy moments throughout the history of the movies. Every single one seems to be there. Claudette Colbert showing Clark Gable how to thumb a ride; Jimmy Durante saying 'What elephant?'; Harold Lloyd hanging from the clock; Chaplin going through the cogs in *Modern Times*, the Marx Brothers in the ship's cabin; the Three Stooges; Laurel and Hardy; Abbott and

Costello; Garbo laughing in *Ninotchka*; Hope and Crosby on the road to everywhere but Samarra; Woody Allen, Mel Brooks . . . the list seems endless. Being the Motion Picture Academy they were given the right to choose what they wanted from any film they liked. I'm happy to say that, as a rare tribute to Peter, the finale of the whole two hours—the scene they chose to finish with—starts with Peter looking at me and saying, 'Does your dog bite?'

A GROUP OF YOUNG AIRMEN

(*To be sung with feeling*)

A group of young airmen,
One night on a camp,
Were talking of sweethearts they had.
They all looked so cheerful,
Excepting one lad,
And he was downhearted and sad.

Cheer up my comrade,
They all cried aloud,
Surely somebody loves you.
But he hung down his head,
And so softly he said,
My comrades I'm love-ed by two.

One has hair of silver and gold,
The other has hair of grey.
One is my mother,
God bless her I love her,
The other is my . . . sweetheart!

(*origin unknown*)

A
Special Coronation Edition
of
'THE GOON SHOW'

---

with

LORD PETER SELLERS
LORD HARRY SECOMBE
LORD SPIKE MILLIGAN
DAME GRAHAM STARK
and
WUFFO, THE WONDER DOG
with
HOO-RAY ELLINGTON AND HIS QUARTET
THE ORCHESTRA CONDUCTED BY SIR WALTER STOTT
ANNOUNCER: ANDREW TIMOTHY
SCRIPT WRITTEN BY THE LATE LARRY STEPHENS AND SPIKE MILLIGAN
EDITED BY COUNCILLOR MAJOR J. D. GRAFTON (CONS.)
PRODUCED BY PISMO CLAM